MW00785615

Eerie
ALABAMA

Eerie ALABAMA

CHILLING TALES FROM THE HEART OF DIXIE

Alan Brown

Illustrations by Kari Schultz

THE
History
PRESS

Published by The History Press
Charleston, SC
www.historypress.com

Copyright © 2019 by Alan Brown
All rights reserved

First published 2019

Manufactured in the United States

ISBN 9781467141673

Library of Congress Control Number: 2019940048

Notice: The information in this book is true and complete to the best of our knowledge. It is offered without guarantee on the part of the author or The History Press. The author and The History Press disclaim all liability in connection with the use of this book.

All rights reserved. No part of this book may be reproduced or transmitted in any form whatsoever without prior written permission from the publisher except in the case of brief quotations embodied in critical articles and reviews.

CONTENTS

Contents

CONTENTS

INTRODUCTION

Storytelling had been an integral part of Alabama's cultural fabric for centuries before its statehood. Alabama's first inhabitants, the Choctaws and Cherokees, passed down tales about geographical landmarks, such as Chewela Creek and Noccalula Falls, and great warriors, such as Tuskaloosa and Tecumseh, for centuries. Tales of Prince Medoc, the great Irish explorer, entered the Native Americans' storytelling traditions around the year 1100 CE. By the end of the 1800s, Alabama's legends were heavily influenced by the contributions of the Scotch-Irish settlers and African American slaves. In the absence of movies and television, storytelling became an important form of entertainment for people living in small towns, big cities and college campuses.

One could argue that folklore collecting in Alabama began with Martha Strudwick Young (1862–1941). She was the daughter of Confederate physician Elisha Young and niece of Alabama reformer Julia Tutwiler. After she graduated from Livingston Female Academy and Normal School, Young embarked on a writing career. In 1884, she began publishing collections of folk tales and legends she had heard from African Americans while growing up in Greensboro, Alabama. Her eight books of folk tales and songs feature black protagonists. Written in black dialect, Young's works, like *Behind the Dark Pines* (1912), established her as a regional writer and allied her with other "dialect" writers, like George Washington Cable and Joel Chandler Harris. By the time she died, Young was known as Alabama's foremost folklorist.

The next serious collector of Alabama's legends was Carl Carmer (1893–1976), who taught at the University of Alabama from 1927 to 1933. During this time, he traveled throughout the state, interviewing the "folk" of Alabama in an attempt to create an accurate picture of the "real" Alabama. Many of his subjects, like Ruby Pickens Tartt from Sumter County, told him tales of outlaws, hood doctors, ex-slaves, folk songs, midwives and Civil War battles. The resulting work, *Stars Fell on Alabama* (1934), became a bestseller, owing its success, in part, to the book's conversational and, at times, poetic style

Although families had been passing down local tales to their children and grandchildren for generations, the preservation of the state's legends and folk tales had not been undertaken on a large scale until the late 1930s. On July 27, 1935, President Franklin Delano Roosevelt signed into law the Federal Writers' Project, which hired over ten thousand clerks, writers, researchers, editors, historians and scholars to collect oral histories, local histories, life histories, city guides, state guides, ethnographies and other works. Many of the interviewers attempted to re-create the storytelling sessions for the reader by faithfully reproducing the dialect. A number of Alabama's signature legends, like "The Face in the Window of the Pickens County Courthouse," first appeared in these collections that eventually found a permanent home in the Library of Congress. An ancillary project, the Slave Narrative Collection, was conducted between 1935 and 1939. The final collection consists of interviews with 2,300 ex-slaves and five hundred photographs.

In the late 1960s, folklore writers presented the legends of Alabama to an entirely new audience by rewriting the standard tales and giving them an artistic flair. One of the most popular of these collections, *13 Alabama Ghosts and Jeffrey* (1969), was written by two Alabama natives, Margaret Gillis Figh (1896–1984) and Kathryn Tucker Windham (1918–2011). This highly successful anthology of thirteen of Alabama's most enduring ghost tales was followed by a number of other successful books, including *Jeffrey's Latest Thirteen* (1982) and *Alabama: One Big Front Porch* (1975). Together, these books are a very loose collection of legends from the entire state.

I had the privilege of knowing Ms. Windham. On our trips from her home in Selma to the main stage at the Sucarnochee Folklife Festival in Livingston, she regaled me with stories about antebellum churches and old diners along Highway 80. On one of our drives, I referred to her as a folklorist, and she immediately corrected me. "I have no formal training as a folklorist," she said. "I'm just a storyteller." It made me sad to think that so many of

Alabama's stories were never published and, therefore, would never be told to future generations.

Eerie Alabama represents my attempt to continue the work that Ms. Windham started in *Alabama: One Big Front Porch* in 1975. Most of these stories would have been perceived by the teller and the listener to be true. Indeed, these tales conform to the Brothers Grimm's definition of a legend being "historically grounded." A few of these stories are updates to Ms. Windham's, such as the chapter on the college legends. Others are closer to mysteries, such as "The Strange Case of Orion Williamson" and "The Disappearance of Harris Rufus Loggins." Only a handful of these legends are probably apocryphal, like the story of Gasparilla the Pirate or the Mobile Leprechaun. One of the most tantalizing aspects of many of the more fantastic tales is the lack of empirical evidence, like in the tale of Alabama's buried giants.

I hope you enjoy this representative sampling of the oral histories of communities spread throughout Alabama. If these versions of the tales differ from the stories you know, keep in mind that they have been embellished over the years through constant retellings. A little piece of the storytellers is reflected in their contributions to the oral tradition. Therefore, there is no single "correct" version of a legend. Because myths and legends are repositories of the state's values, history and geography, they should all ring with a note of familiarity.

I

MYSTERIOUS MONSTERS

THE "WHITE THANG" OF ALABAMA

For generations, people have associated "Bigfoot" with the Pacific Northwest, where native tribes relayed tales of "hairy men" years before the arrival of white settlers. Indians living in North America had more than sixty different words for the monster. In the 1840s, Native Americans living near present-day Spokane, Washington, told missionaries stories of a larger-than-life creature that lived in the mountains and stole salmon from their nets. In the 1920s, a Canadian newspaper reporter gave the creature a name—"Sasquatch," an anglicized form of a Halkomelem Indian word meaning "wild man." Interestingly enough, only one-third of all Bigfoot-sighting claims have been located in the Pacific Northwest. Bigfoot sightings have also been reported in the Great Lakes region and in the southeastern United States. In 1972, the movie *The Legend of Boggy Creek* brought national attention to the Fouke Monster, which has been seen in and around Fouke, Arkansas, since the 1950s. Other southern versions of Bigfoot include the Skunk Ape and the Cabbage Man, which are said to roam the wilds of Florida and Louisiana. According to the Alabama Bigfoot Society, a number of different Bigfoot sightings have been reported in Alabama since 2014. However, the state's most famous Bigfoot is the "White Thang."

Sightings of the "White Thang" in central Alabama date back to the 1930s. Many witnesses described it as a large, white, man-like creature that walked on all fours. Others claimed that the monster walked upright and was seven feet tall. The "White Thang" was said to climb trees and scream at people as they walked underneath. To date, no detailed descriptions of the creature's facial features have surfaced.

Several reports of albino, Sasquatch-like creatures have been posted on the Alabama Bigfoot Society's website. On July 15, 2016, witnesses filmed a large, man-like creature striding along a ridge in Wood Knock Hollow in Clay County. The video of the snow-white figure has been posted on YouTube. On the website werewolves. com, a man named Wayne Miller says that one summer night, when he was a boy, he heard a loud noise in the yard. The old lady who lived next door grabbed her garden hoe and ran outside to confront whatever was causing the racket, despite the fact that her normally aggressive German shepherd lay whimpering on the front porch. She charged down the path toward her garden where the creature she recognized as the "White Thang" was helping himself to her vegetables. She scared the creature as much as it scared her, and it ran past her on all fours. Wayne says he regrets having slept through the excitement.

In 2013, a woman living in Blount County had an even more terrifying encounter with the "White Thang." She and her family had just moved into an old house that they had planned on renovating. The house was situated in an overgrown area north of Oneonta. A nearby creek made this an ideal habitat for a humanoid creature. On this particular day, at noon, she and her husband were cleaning up the front yard, and their son was walking around to the back of the house. Suddenly, he ran back to the front of the house, shouting that a white-haired monster was in a ditch. The boy said that he made eye contact with the creature before it slowly walked into the woods. After the frightened boy calmed down, he recalled that the beast's long, white hair covered its eyes, concealing its facial features. He estimated that it stood around nine feet tall.

The "White Thang" is not the only Bigfoot reputed to be roaming the woods of Alabama, but it is undoubtedly the most distinctive because of its white hair. Some researchers have speculated that the "White Thang" is actually an albino Bigfoot. Unless one of the elusive animals is either captured or killed, we will never know.

THE DOWNEY BOOGER

In the late nineteenth century, a number of Bigfoot-like sightings were reported in Winston County. Known as the "Downey Booger," this half-human, half-simian creature was spotted in some of the county's less-populated areas. Joyce Farris, whose husband's ancestors, the Downey family, encountered the beast, published an account by another descendant of the Downey family, Vera Whitehead, on Winston County's website, freestateofwinston.org. Late one night in the 1890s, two cousins, John and Joe Downey, were riding their horses home from a dance held at the house owned by a man named Oscar Tittle. All at once, a hairy, anthropoid-type beast appeared in the middle of the road. The horses reared back in fear, almost jostling the riders from their saddles, and headed back toward Tittle's log house. With a great deal of effort, the young men stopped the horses and turned them around. When the horses reached the sand bed where the creature had appeared, they came to an abrupt halt. No amount of prodding from the riders could entice them to go any farther. Reluctantly, the boys returned to the Tittle house along Byler Road. By the time they finally made it home, the sun had risen over the horizon. Their terrified demeanor could not convince their parents that they had really seen a monster. Unknown to the boys, they had given a name to a creature that was seen on at least two other occasions.

Three months later, another family from the same part of Winston County was returning from church along the same road where the Downey cousins had their sighting when a large, hairy creature emerged from a clump of

bushes along the sand bed. For just a few seconds, the monster stared at the terrified family before darting back into the bushes. The children were so frightened by their experience that they slept on a pallet in their parents' bedroom for several months.

In the fall of the same year, a local moonshiner named Jim Jackson was driving a wagon loaded with several barrels of whiskey to Galloway, where he hoped to sell his load to the town's thirsty miners. The moonshiner was riding along, thinking of the profit he would make from the commissary, when he was overcome by a feeling of unease. When he turned around, he was shocked to see that he was being followed by an inhuman "thing" that was loping behind the wagon at an easy pace. Jackson considered trying to outrun it, but his mules were unaccustomed to running on level ground. Out of desperation, he grabbed a revolver and fired twice at the shadowy figure. Afterward, he reported that it "screamed like a woman" as it hurriedly limped away. That same week, a posse searched the entire area only to find a few patches of blood leading from the sand pit to a cliff. No one knows whether or not Jackson killed his pursuer. Without a doubt, the Downey Booger has acquired a second life in the lore of Winston County.

THE WOLF WOMAN OF MOBILE

Mobile, Alabama, is one of the oldest and most colorful cities in the United States. Mobile was founded as a French settlement on Twenty-Seven Mile Bluff by Pierre Le Moyne d'Iberville under the name Fort Louis de la Louisiane. The settlement was established in 1702 as the first capital of colonial New France by his brother, Jean-Baptiste Le Moy, Sieur de Bienville, who had been appointed governor of the French colony of Louisiana in 1701. The bishop of Quebec, Jean-Baptiste de la Croix de Chevrieres de Saint-Vallier, established Mobile's Roman Catholic parish on July 20, 1703. A year later, twenty-three young women were brought to Mobile by a ship, the *Pelican*, to become wives of the colonists. They were called "casquette girls" because of the odd shape of their hope chests. Mobile remained a part of New France until 1763, when it became a part of the "fourteenth British colony": West Florida. Today, evidence of the French influence can be seen in Mobile's street names, French cuisine, architecture and folklore.

One French legend that appears to have migrated from Louisiana to Mobile is the myth of the rougarou, which is a Cajun variant of the *loup-garou*, which means "werewolf" in French. The legend was carried down to southern Louisiana by the French settlers and by the French-Canadian immigrants. The rougarou is typically described as a hybrid creature with the body of a human being and the head of a wolf. Cajun children were warned that the rougarou would "get them" if they ventured outside after dark. Many Cajuns believed that people who violated the rules of Lent were turned into rougarous and were then given a mission to kill other people who failed to observe Lent properly. According to another variant of the legend, the accursed person retains the shape of a wolf for 101 days, after which the creature's victims also become rougarous. In yet another version of the legend, witches have the ability to transform themselves and other people into rougarous.

Interestingly enough, the Cajun legend of the rougarou seems to have made its way to Mobile, Alabama, in the twentieth century. On April 8, 1971, the *Mobile Press-Register* reported that the newspaper's office had received over fifty phone calls regarding a strange creature with the upper body of a woman and the hindquarters of a wolf. One witness described the creature as "pretty and hairy." Another was quoted as saying, "My daughter saw it down in a marsh, and it chased her home. Now, my mommy keeps all the doors and windows locked." The *Press-Register* reporter added, "None of the callers who volunteered descriptive information on the 'wolf woman' had personally seen it, but they all had close friends and relatives who had." The apparition evidently frequents Davis Avenue and Plateau Street after nightfall. The Mobile police department, which was also receiving phone calls about the beast, investigated a number of the reports but found no hard evidence of the creature's existence.

When the reports of the "wolf woman" died down ten days after they began, a number of theories were generated by way of explaining the creature's sudden appearance. One resident of Mobile believed that the monster was a fugitive from a circus sideshow. Others believed that the "wolf woman" was actually a Native American shape-shifter or "skin walker" who possessed the power to change into the shape of an animal at will. However, one should not ignore the close proximity between the timing the "wolf woman" sightings and April Fool's Day.

MOBILE'S LEPRECHAUN SIGHTING

Leprechauns are the most iconic characters in Irish folklore. The first leprechauns were water spirits known as *luchorpan*, which means "small body." These war-like fairies were driven by their appetites, especially the females, who lured men away from their wives and girlfriends. In 1604, these mischievous spirits first appeared in print as "lubricans" in Thomas Dekker's comedy *The Honest Whore, Part 2*. Another early name for these creatures was *leath bhrogan*, which connected them to the shoe-making profession. It is said that one could detect the presence of these sprightly cobblers by the tapping sound of their hammers. Supposedly, leprechauns are always in need of shoes because they enjoy dancing. Originally, the typical leprechaun was portrayed as wearing a red, square-cut coat. Then in 1825, T. Crofton Croker's *Fairy Traditions and Legends of the South of Ireland* presented the standard depiction of leprechauns as solitary old men who stand between two and three feet tall and wear green clothes and buckled shoes. Some leprechauns smoke a pipe and wear pointed caps. Croker said they were vain creatures who took great pride in their appearance. Their jackets have seven rows of buttons with seven buttons in each row. Leprechauns are rarely seen because they spend most of their time in hollow trees or underground caves. Probably the best-known leprechaun legend is the pot of gold that the leprechauns have hidden at the end of a rainbow. Because cobbling is not a very lucrative profession, their pot of gold consists of gold coins they found under the ground. They are devious creatures who easily elude capture by using their pursuers' greed against them. However, any human being fortunate enough to catch them is granted three wishes. In the twentieth century, leprechauns have morphed into the cartoonish spokesperson for Lucky Charms cereal and as Notre Dame's mascot. As portrayed in the films by Warwick Davis, the leprechaun has become a vengeful demon who delights in torturing those foolish enough to steal his gold.

Ireland is generally considered to be the best place to spot a leprechaun. However, one of the most humorous sightings occurred in the Mobile neighborhood of Crichton. On March 14, 2006, WPMI-TV reporter Brian Johnson was sent to Crichton to investigate the appearance of a leprechaun. When the television crew arrived in Crichton, they were told by a number of people that a leprechaun was sighted in a tree. One of the people Johnson interviewed, Demarco Morrisette, showed the reporter a special "leprechaun flute" that, supposedly, was thousands of years old. Another resident of the neighborhood speculated that the so-called leprechaun "could be a crackhead that got ahold of the wrong stuff" and was told to pretend to be a leprechaun. Another Crichton resident—Nina Thomas-

Brown—showed Johnson a sketch she had drawn of the leprechaun. Several "witnesses" seemed to be more concerned about the possibility that a pot of gold lay buried under the tree. A plan by one of Crichton's residents to use a backhoe to dig up the gold has still not come to fruition. Afterward, Johnson expressed skepticism that the leprechaun was real, suggesting that it might have been a shadowy image formed by branches and hanging Spanish moss.

WPMI-TV aired the segment that evening and once again on the morning show. On March 17, user "botmib" posted the segment on YouTube, and it became one of the site's first viral sensations. As I write this, the YouTube video has received over twenty-one million views. The video was so popular, in fact, that some people credit it with helping to launch YouTube. Over the next few months, the video seemed to be everywhere. "Shock jock" Howard Stern and a *New York Times* columnist also contributed to the hoopla surrounding the video. Fox News' Bill O'Reilly examined the racist dimensions of the video. Even *South Park* and *The Daily Show* lampooned the video. It remains one of late-night talk show host Jimmy Kimmel's favorite viral news stories. One can be certain that every St. Patrick's Day, the Mobile leprechaun video will be airing somewhere.

ALABAMA'S HOGZILLA—REAL OR FAKE?

The original Hogzilla was a hybrid of a domestic pig and wild hog. On June 17, 2004, Chris Griffin shot the enormous boar on Ken Holyoak's fish farm and hunting reserve in Alapaha, Georgia. Griffin measured and weighed the hog before burying it. He claimed that it was 12 feet long and weighed over one thousand pounds. One year later, forensic scientists exhumed the pig for a National Geographic documentary. They determined that Hogzilla was between 6.9 and 8.6 feet long and that it really weighed eight hundred pounds. Despite the hog's diminished dimensions, it is still known as the one and only "Hogzilla." However, in 2007, a challenger to that title surfaced in Alabama.

On May 26, 2007, foxnews.com published the story of an amazing hunt in Alabama. On May 3, 2007, Jamison Stone, an eleven-year-old boy from Pickensville, Alabama, killed a huge feral pig at the Lost Creek Plantation using a .50-caliber Smith & Wesson. The boy said that after tracking the hog for three hours, he finished it off with a shot to the head in a creek bed. His father, Mike Stone, and two guides shadowed the boy with high-powered rifles in the event that the hog charged at Jamison with its five-inch tusks. With a great deal of effort, the men loaded the hog onto a truck and transported it to the Clay County Farmers Exchange. The nine-foot-four-inch-long beast weighed 1,051 pounds. A local taxidermist named Jerry Cunningham told a reporter for the *Anniston Star*, "It was the biggest thing I'd ever seen." Cunningham mounted the massive head on an extra-large foam form. Mike Stone predicted that the remainder of the hog would produce between 500 and 700 pounds of sausage. A photograph of the boy posing with the slain swine received national attention. The amazing animal catapulted Jamison Stone into fame. A host of celebrities, including country music star Kenny Chesney, sent the boy their congratulations.

The boy's claim soon proved to be short-lived. Suspecting a hoax, NBC canceled an interview with the Stones. Retired New York University physicist Dr. Richard Brandt determined that the boy was actually standing several feet behind the hog to exaggerate the size of the beast, and a number of photography experts also concluded that the photograph had been digitally altered. At the same time the authenticity of the photograph was being examined, several reporters began probing into the truth behind the hunt itself. It turned out that the "monster hog" was actually a domestic pig named Fred that lived on a nearby farm. The owners of the pig, Rhonda and Phil Blissitt, sold the pig to Eddy Borden, the owner of Lost Creek Plantation, to draw attention to his hunting preserve. In January 2008, an Alabama grand jury began its investigation of the owners of Southeastern Trophy Hunters, Eddy Borden, Keith O'Neal and Charles Williams. In media reports, Borden was accused of buying Fred from the Blissitts for $500 and then duping the Stones into thinking it was a wild hog. The investigation stood on the grounds that allowing an eleven-year-old boy to pump bullets into the hog until it bled out constituted cruelty to animals. Alabama's attorney general, Troy King, told Rhonda Roland Shearer, the director of Art Science Research Laboratory, that his office did not have the time to pursue the case before the statute of limitations expired on May 3, 2008. The grand jury was canceled by Clay County district attorney Fred Thomson without explanation.

THE COOSA RIVER MONSTER

Even though the Coosa River is a tributary of the Alabama River, it stretches approximately 280 miles through Georgia and Alabama. Before entering Alabama at Weiss Lake, the Coosa River begins at the confluence of the Etowah and Dostanauta Rivers in Rome, Georgia. The Coosa River ends just north of Montgomery. Most of the Coosa River flows through Alabama. Thanks to the runoff of nutrients from different forms of land use, the Coosa River is very fertile. In Alabama, the Coosa River is home to a variety of fish, snails, mussels and, some people say, a river monster.

According to the *Gadsden Times*, the first sighting of a weird aquatic beast occurred in 1816. The writer of a letter to the editor told the seemingly apocryphal tale of a dying monster that was discovered half-submerged near Ten Islands, Alabama. A group of curious settlers cut the creature open and were shocked to find the partially digested remains of a deer, an Indian, his weapons and an entire canoe. One of the spectators speculated that the monster had died after eating the Indian's rifle.

The sightings escalated after 1845 when riverboats began bringing passengers and goods to the area. In 1862, the river monster surfaced once again in the pages of the *Gadsden Times*. The first witness was a pioneer named Mrs. Marin, who claimed to have seen a snake-like creature floating on the surface of the water. A few months later, two of Cherokee County's most highly esteemed citizens—Judge Lemuel Standifer and Captain J.M. Eliott—sighted the creature swimming in the river near Rome, Georgia.

On June 8, 1877, the *Gadsden Times* ran a story about a prominent citizen named Marcus Foster, who was in a boat running a trotline near Ball Play

THE GREAT SEA SERPENT
(according to Hans Egede.)

This 1734 illustration of a sea serpent by Hans Egede is very similar to the eyewitness descriptions of the Coosa River Monster, a serpentine creature with a horse-shaped head. *R. Ellis.*

Creek when he spotted what seemed to be a boat floating near the opposite bank and paddled closer to the object. When Foster was fifty yards away, he thought he was looking at a woman standing waist-high in the water. As Foster moved even closer, the mysterious object revealed itself as a large, serpent-like creature with a horse-like head. Foster distinctly recalled that the monster had large, bulging eyes and a long, red tongue. Panic-stricken, the fisherman rowed away as fast as he could. When he was a safe distance away from the creature, Foster paused to watch it lazily drift along the shore until it sank into the murky depths of the river.

The last reported sighting of the Coosa River Monster took place in June 1882. The *Gadsden Times* reporter who saw the monster said that he was rowing along the Coosa River when, all at once, a large, amorphous mass bubbled up to the surface, directly in front of his boat. On close observation, the reporter noted that the bizarre "beast" was actually a large clump of grass and leaves that had been propelled to the surface by bubbles of methane gas. The reporter was convinced that he had debunked all of the previous sightings of the Coosa River Monster. The number of sightings fell off dramatically until the 1950s.

A composite of the Coosa River Monster can be derived from *Gadsden Times* articles dating back to the 1800s. Witnesses described the serpentine monster as being between fifteen and twenty feet long and covered with scales and fins. The monster always disappeared under the water when it sensed that someone was watching it.

Alabama's Fossilized Sea Serpent

In the first half of the nineteenth century, a number of sightings of sea serpents were being reported in Alabama, especially in the Tennessee River. Ironically, the bones of a real sea serpent were discovered around this same time. In 1832, the vertebra of a prehistoric creature was sent from Louisiana to the American Philosophical Society in Philadelphia. Two years later, natural historian Richard Harlan published a report in which he named the animal *Basilosaurus*, or "king lizard." Judge John C. Creagh from Clarke County sent Harlan additional *Basilosaurus* bones, including teeth and jaw bones. In 1839, Harlan transported the fossils to England so that they could be examined by Richard Owens, who had been conducting research on a group of large ancient reptiles he called "Dinosauria." Owens concluded that because the teeth were double-rooted, they belonged to a mammal, probably a prehistoric whale, which he called "Zeuglodon." However, Owens's name for the Eocene whale did not replace Harlan's original name.

The discovery of a prehistoric whale in southern Alabama created a sensation in the media. In 1845, a showman from Missouri named Howard Koch concocted a scheme to exploit the public's fascination with *Basilosaurus*.

Basilosaurus cetoides, a prehistoric whale that lived forty to thirty-five million years ago, is the official state fossil of Alabama. *Alan Brown.*

He traveled to Alabama and purchased a number of *Basilosaurus* bones. He then assembled a fantastic sea creature he called an "immense antediluvian monster." While the public flocked to see Koch's 114-foot-long hodgepodge of bones and newspaper reviews were generally favorable, scientists were skeptical. A group of experts who inspected the bones denounced Koch's sea serpent as a fraud.

Today, *Basilosaurus cetoides* is classified as a seventy-foot-long whale that lived forty-five million years ago in a shallow sea near the Gulf of Mexico. Fossilized skeletons of the prehistoric whale are on display at the McWane Science Center in Birmingham, the Smithsonian, the University of Southern Mississippi in Hattiesburg and the University of Alabama in Tuscaloosa. Another *Basilosaurus cetoides* skeleton was unearthed in Washington County in 1982, and the Alabama State Legislature designated *Basilosaurus cetoides* as Alabama's state fossil in 1984.

ALABAMA'S WAMPUS CAT

The Wampus Cat is generally considered to be an Appalachian folk tale. Several variants of the legend exist, but the best known is from Tennessee. The story says that years ago, a beautiful Native American woman burned with curiosity regarding her husband's hunting trips with the other men of the tribe. At the time, women were forbidden to accompany their husbands on forays into the woods. One evening, she wrapped herself in a mountain lion skin to keep warm and followed her husband and the other men. Hiding behind a rock, she witnessed the tribe's magic rites and overheard the storytelling sessions. Suddenly, one of the men saw her, and she was brought out into the open. The medicine man punished her by transforming her into the beast whose skin she was wearing. The half-woman, half–mountain lion was condemned to a solitary existence, wandering through the forest for eternity. The creature ran into the woods and howled to express her desire to return to human form.

The first person to see the Wampus Cat was a man who was hunting with his dogs. He had not gone very far when he detected the pungent smell of what seemed to be an animal that had fallen into a bog and soaked its fur. All at once, the man heard something howling behind him. He spun around and found himself staring into the yellow eyes of the Wampus Cat. The man jumped backward and ran through the woods with the Wampus Cat right behind him. Almost out of breath, he finally reached his cabin. The hunter dashed inside and slammed the door shut behind him. While the Wampus Cat threw its weight against the door, the man picked up his Bible and began reading from the book of Psalms. After a few minutes, the Wampus Cat ran off, apparently repelled by the holy words of the Bible.

Alabama has its own variant of the Wampus Cat legend that bears little resemblance to the Appalachian version. According to Mike Conley's *Tales of the Weird: Legend of the Wampus Cat*, the federal government conducted a series of experiments in the Alabama backwoods to create a swift-running beast that could be used as a messenger during World War II. The beast was a mixture of mountain lion and gray wolf. Unfortunately, fate intervened. Somehow, a number of the animals escaped their confinement and ran off into the woods. Descendants of these feline and canine hybrids are said to have attacked livestock and robbed chicken coops throughout the state. Sightings of Alabama's Wampus Cat have been reported as far north as the Great Smoky Mountains and as far south as the Florida Everglades.

In her book *Myths, Mysteries & Legends of Alabama*, author Elaine Hobson Miller told the story of an encounter a sixteen-year-old boy named John Rowell had with a Wampus Cat while hunting rabbits in the New Cahaba Cemetery in 1980. Interestingly enough, Rowell's tale has more in common with the Appalachian Wampus Cat legends of the nineteenth century than with the Alabama variant. He was riding on the hood of his 1956 Mercury, holding his .22-caliber rifle, when he heard a sound that sent shivers down his spine: "It was a high-pitched sound, sort of a cross between a panther and a woman screaming. We took off, and that was our introduction to the Wampus Cat." Rowell and his friend made several nighttime visits to the New Cahaba Cemetery, sometimes out of boredom, but mostly because they wanted to see the creature that had made their blood run cold. He learned to call up the Wampus Cat by imitating its wail.

One night while Rowell and his buddies were sitting in their convertible and calling up the giant feline, they heard it walk through the brush and bang against the fence. They suddenly felt something huge try to climb up the back of the car. Rowell's fear overcame his curiosity, and he gunned the engine to take off. When the boys had driven a safe distance away from the beast, they stopped the car and walked around to the back. Rowell was amazed to see two large claw-like scratches in the frost on the trunk, between eight and ten inches wide.

In much of the Deep South, the term "Wampus Cat" is used to refer to any large, unknown feline. In many cases, the Wampus Cat is a panther. However, people who have actually encountered a Wampus Cat, like John Rowell, will tell you that there is no comparison between a panther and a real Wampus Cat.

THE BELL WITCH IN ALABAMA

The story of the Bell Witch is one of the American Southeast's best-known legends. In 1804, John Bell moved from Halifax County, North Carolina, to one hundred acres of land near a settlement that later came to be known at Adams Station. Over the next decade, John and his wife spent most of their time working on the farm and raising their eight children. Their lives became the stuff of folklore in 1817 when a vengeful woman named Kate Batts entered their lives. The "bad blood" between them can be traced back to a business deal in which Bell sold Batts a slave and charged her excessive interest. Before long, the family heard a number of blood-curdling sounds inside the house, including knocking, scratching and the smacking of lips. Bell's daughter, Betsy, complained of being pinched and slapped by an unseen hand. The haunting of the Bell family gained widespread notoriety following an investigation of the house by a neighbor and friend, James Johnston, and his son, John, both of whom claimed to have had conversations with the entity. Following his victory at the Battle of New Orleans, Andrew Jackson visited the Bell family. He and his entourage were about a mile from the farm when his wagon inexplicably stopped moving. After Jackson blamed the strange occurrence on Kate Batts, the men heard a spectral voice say, "You may continue, gentlemen." For some reason, the spirit was kind toward John's wife and sang hymns and even brought her bowls of fruit. However, over time, Batts's hatred of John Bell intensified. At one point, she cursed Bell, whom she referred to as "Old Jack," and even vowed to kill him. She carried through with her promise in 1820 when Bell died from poisoning. Batts even interrupted Bell's funeral by singing drinking songs. Seven years later, the revenant returned, tormenting Lucy and her sons Richard and Joel. Although John Bell's persecution by the Bell Witch is generally considered to be inextricably associated with Tennessee, one particularly bizarre element of the story has an Alabama connection as well.

John Bell first realized that an otherworldly force had entered his life in 1817 while walking through his cornfield. Suddenly, a large animal appeared in front of Bell. Later, Bell told his wife Lucy that, at first sight, the beast seemed to be a mongrel dog with patches of white on its back and chest. It had very large paws, and its tail was just a puff of fur. As Bell continued staring at the creature, he realized that it had the head of a large jackrabbit with ears that stood up straight. He aimed his rifle at the thing and fired, but it bound away unharmed, even though the shot was at close range. Shaking his head, Bell said that the animal ran faster than any dog he had ever seen.

A century later, the weird canine reappeared in Florence, Alabama, according to an article that appeared in the *Montgomery Advertiser* on February 25, 1912:

> *The Bell witch, which many years ago brought terror and destruction to an East Tennessee family, has reappeared, this time in Blackburn beat [in] Lauderdale County, according to the belief of some residents of that place. The story has reached Florence that a strange animal is seen roaming in that section which resembles a large dog, but the most terrifying part of it is its scream. This can be heard for a mile or more and resembles the scream of a woman in terror. The animal is reddish brown color with a white streak about its throat. Few have seen it, but many have heard it, and the*

Located at the site of John Bell's farm, this replica of John Bell's cabin contains furnishings from the time he lived there with his family. *Brian Stansberry.*

boldest are afraid to be abroad after dark. Remembering the sad fate of Judge Bell, no one has had [the] courage to shoot at the animal. Squire Silas L. Bradley of Blackburn beat, who was a recent visitor to Florence, is convinced that a deep mystery surrounds the strange animal.

Some parapsychologists believe the sightings of the dog-beast are proof that Kate Batts was a shape-shifter who possessed the ability to transform herself into an animal, much like a werewolf or vampire. Why she decided to manifest in Alabama is anybody's guess.

TWO-TOED TOM: ALABAMA'S MONSTER ALLIGATOR

People living in the southern parts of Alabama and Florida began swapping tales about a monstrous alligator that ate their mules, cows, dogs and even other people. They described it as a "red-eyed demon" approximately fifteen feet long. Its name, "Two-Toed Tom," was derived from the alligator's distinctive footprints. One of Tom's feet had only two toes because he had gotten caught in a trap. When Carl Carmer visited the area in 1934 to conduct research for his book *Stars Fell on Alabama*, locals told him that, unlike most alligators, which were shy, Two-Toed Tom aggressively attacked—and ate—people and livestock. He knocked cattle and horses off their feet with a sweep of his massive tail. Some people believed that the alligator was a hellish creature sent by the devil. Two-Toed Tom was even accused of hunting down and raping women from time to time.

The best-known encounter with Two-Toed Tom involved a farmer named Pap Haines. After putting up with the reptilian marauder for twenty years, Haines finally lost his patience when Two-Toed Tom killed his favorite mule. He and his son, with a posse of eight men, filled fifteen syrup buckets with dynamite and tossed them in the pool that they thought was Tom's home. The resulting explosion rent the air with dead fish and clumps of mud. Trees lining the pond were entirely uprooted. Before the smoke cleared, Haynes heard the sound of screaming from the vicinity of an adjacent pond. When Haines and his son reached the site of the screaming, they were horrified by what they saw. Haines's twelve-year-old daughter had been ripped to pieces on the shore.

Haines spent the rest of his life hunting for the beast that had killed his daughter, not knowing that the beast's survival instinct had driven it into Florida following the explosion. Two-Toed Tom was sighted on farms and in settlements along the Choctawhatchee River and the Holmes Creek swamps. People living in the town of Esto claimed to have seen him basking on the shore of Sand Hammock Lake. A group of boys who saw him at the lake swore that he was between eighteen and twenty-four feet long. Many witnesses said his thunderous bellows could be heard echoing through the night air. Every night, he roared when the whistle signaled shift changes at the Alabama-Florida Lumber Company. The most frightening encounter in this region occurred when a mother and her little girl were walking along the shore of Sand Hammock. As the little girl played in the sand a few feet away, her mother gasped as a huge alligator emerged from bushes and raised up on its hind legs behind her daughter. The screams of the mother and her daughter and the roar of the alligator drew a group of armed men to the scene. They continued firing round after round into the monster until its movements ceased. After they summoned up the courage to walk toward the beast and inspect it, Two-Toed Tom got up and swept the men off their feet with his tail.

One of the legends Carl Carmer included in his book *Stars Fell in Alabama* is the story of "Two-Toed Tom," a monstrous alligator that prowled the swamps of southeast and southwest Alabama in the 1930s. *Clement Bardot.*

Not long after the publication of Carmer's book, sightings of Two-Toed Tom began to diminish in number. Then in the 1980s, memories of the vicious predator resurfaced following the discovery of a huge alligator "slide," or path, on Boyton Island on the Choctawhatchee River. The footprints revealed that one of the alligator's feet had only two toes. The resulting media frenzy, which included a mention on the *NBC Evening News*, resulted in an extensive hunt for the legendary animal, with no success. Considering that the average lifespan of an alligator living in the wild is between thirty and fifty years, Two-Toed Tom would have had to have led a charmed life to be as old as people say. Even today, sightings of the massive creature are reported in the swamps of eastern Florida.

HUGGIN' MOLLY

Abbeville is a small agricultural city in Henry County and is located in what has come to be known as Alabama's Wiregrass Region. Abbeville was called *Yalta Abba*—"grove of Dogwoods"—by the Creek Indians; to this day,

Abbeville is known to many people as "The City of Dogwoods." However, generations of children growing up in Abbeville have viewed their little town as the home of a phantom named "Huggin' Molly."

"Huggin Molly" is a cautionary tale that was most likely told to children in the twentieth century to prevent them from venturing out late at night. In the standard version, "Huggin' Molly" crept up behind a bad boy or girl and wrapped the errant child in an embrace so tight that breathing became impossible. In a less common variant, "Huggin' Molly" grabbed disobedient children and screamed in their ears. Abbeville resident Jimmy Rane said that his relatives told him the tale to keep him from breaking curfew. "If your mother and dad didn't want you to be out after dark, they'd tell you Huggin' Molly would get you."

Many adult residents, who believed as children that the entity was chasing them, now realize that their imaginations had gotten the best of them. However, two men who spent their childhoods in Abbeville are certain that their chance meetings with "Huggin' Molly" were real. Mack Gregory told an interviewer in 1960 that when he was a teenager, he had just finished delivering groceries late one evening and was walking home on East Washington Street after dark when he suddenly sensed that he was being followed. He turned around and was shocked to see a figure dressed in black walking just a few steps behind him. He started running and did not stop until he was safe inside his front door. James Robert Shell's encounter, which occurred in the 1920s, was similar. He was returning home late one night on the corner of Elm and Clendinen Streets when he was also followed by a strange creature in a black robe. Once he caught a glimpse of what was behind him, Shell took off running. When he was one hundred yards from his house, he saw his mother standing on the porch, holding the front door open for him. "Run, Robert, run!" she yelled at the top of her voice. Shell credited his mother with saving his life that night.

Like many small towns in Alabama, Abbeville celebrates its legend. One of the town's most popular restaurants, Huggin' Molly's, takes its name from the local phantom. Even Abbeville's welcome sign features the silhouette of a witch-like woman chasing a little boy. Clearly, Abbeville has learned to live with the creature that still strikes fear in the hearts of children.

II

UNDERWATER MYSTERIES

CATZILLA: JUST ANOTHER FISH STORY?

Tales of monstrous creatures in Alabama's waterways, especially the Coosa River, were prevalent throughout much of the nineteenth century. During the nineteenth and early twentieth centuries, a number of people reported seeing a catfish that weighed over two hundred pounds. After the construction of the dams along the Coosa and Tennessee Rivers in the early 1900s, the number of giant fish sightings increased exponentially. In the 1950s, a creature by the name of "Catzilla" surfaced in the river lore of the state. Witnesses claimed that the Tennessee River had spawned an enormous catfish that was as large as a Volkswagon Beetle.

These sightings raise an important question: are the Coosa and Tennessee Rivers home to a car-size catfish capable of swallowing a human being? Dr. Zeb Hogan, host of the National Geographic WILD show *Monster Fish*, devoted an entire episode to exploring the possibility that giant fish inhabit the rivers of the American South. Dr. Hogan said that the world-record-holding blue catfish, which weighed in at 143 pounds, was caught in North Carolina in 2003. Car-sized catfish have only been caught in exotic locales. For example, in 2010, a nine-foot-long catfish weighing 646 pounds was caught in Thailand. According to Dr. Hogan, two dozen varieties of freshwater fish reach gigantic proportions: "There are two dozen species of freshwater fish larger than six feet and weighing more than 200 pounds, which is as big as a person, and some weigh up to 600 or 700 pounds." Hogan believes that some species of fish in Alabama were much bigger in the nineteenth century before the intrusion of human beings and chemicals. The giant fish that so many people encountered in the Coosa and Tennessee Rivers in the 1800s could have possibly been some of these enormous catfish. Catzilla, then, may have disappeared in the twentieth century once civilization and its detrimental effects on the fish's habitat were firmly in place.

Lake Martin's Drowned Towns

In the early 1900s, engineers were investigating Cherokee Bluffs, where the Tallapoosa River flows through the ridge, as a possible dam site. They determined that Cherokee Bluffs would be an ideal location for a dam because the narrow river flowed over rock and was enclosed by bluffs on both sides. In addition, the area was sparsely inhabited. In 1916, the Alabama Power Company received permission to build the dam. However, the actual construction of the dam was delayed until 1923 because of the advent of World War I. The ambitious project soon proved to be challenging to say the least. Once sixty thousand acres were acquired, bridges, roads, cemeteries and people had to be relocated. Over one thousand workers were hired to clear the land, and a railroad spur was constructed to facilitate the transportation of materials.

Two African American communities were submerged when the Lake Martin Dam was built in 1926. Benson was founded in 1895 by Will Benson. Susannah, also known as "Sousana," was a bustling little town that included a gristmill, a flour mill, a gold mine, a church, a school, a blacksmith shop and two mercantile shops. Before the land was flooded, over nine hundred bodies were removed from the cemetery, but neither of the towns was relocated.

Most of the buildings in Benson and Susannah were dismantled before the dam was completed to ensure that the lake would be free of hazards. Nevertheless, people swimming and boating on Lake Martin have claimed to hear the tolling of the bell of the submerged church. Because the graves of coon dogs were not moved before the land was flooded, the baying of their unquiet spirits is also said to echo across the lake on moonlit nights.

DOES A WORLD WAR II–ERA AIRPLANE LIE UNDER LAKE MARTIN?

Lake Martin's submerged towns entered the realm of folklore in the 1920s and 1930s. However, in the mid-1940s, people in the surrounding area began talking about another sunken secret at the bottom of the lake. On March 20, 1945, a B-25 bomber was flying from Washington, D.C., to Texas on a training mission for the United States Army. On board were the pilot, Captain John Glen Mabry, and two passengers, Captain Charles P. Oliver, who lived in Penacock, New Jersey, and Staff Sergeant James N. Green, an aerial engineer from Washington, D.C. Captain Mabry was an experienced pilot who had accumulated four hundred hours of flying time in B-25s. At 10:30 a.m., Captain Mabry piloted the B-25 to Atlanta, Georgia, for a routine maintenance check. He had planned on flying to Maxwell Air Force Base in Montgomery, Alabama, to refuel, but the plane never made it that far. That same day, Alabama was buffeted by severe thunderstorms, which spawned two tornadoes.

For three days, over two dozen planes from Maxwell Air Force Base and Gunter Annex searched a fifty-mile grid from Montgomery to Atlanta. Pieces of the wreckage from the B-25 were eventually spotted by officials at Sand Mountain, which is not far from Lake Martin. Only Sergeant Green's body was recovered, along with a few pieces of the plane and several life preservers. The Army Air Report, based on photographs of the debris recovered from Lake Martin and Boling Airfield, did not include a cause for the crash of the twenty-two-thousand-pound aircraft. However, former aircraft mechanic Bobby Norwood theorized that the right engine caught fire, and the alcohol tank exploded: "It got all smoky in the cockpit…and I believe they got disoriented and went right in [the lake]." Muddy conditions in the lake made retrieval of the plane impossible.

After a while, the crash of the B-25 faded from public memory. Then in the early 1990s, Bobby Norwood decided to do his best to retrieve the plane. Using depth finders, metal detectors and information supplied by locals, Norwood combed the lake. A small article in the 1945 *Dadeville Record* enabled Norwood to find the exact point of impact near Sandy Creek. Norwood began an extensive search of the area. "We had been searching for two years, every weekend, even through the winter. It was 35 degrees, and we were out there diving. That's how the whole project has been. Since we started diving, I haven't done anything on the weekends but come up here and work on it," Norwood said. Finally, in 1992, Norwood's hard work paid

Manufactured by North American Aviation, the twin-engine B-25 Mitchell bomber flew in every theater of World War II. *Lukas Skywalker.*

off. One day, his diving partner retrieved a mud-encrusted piece of metal with a rivet hole. This seemingly inconspicuous find proved to be the first piece of the B-25 to see the light of day in forty-six years. The duo had done more than simply locate the wreckage of an old airplane. They had revived interest in a tragic footnote from World War II.

ALABAMA'S UNDERWATER FOREST

Hurricane Katrina will be remembered primarily for the devastation it wrought over the coastal areas of the Deep South in 2005. However, the massive storm also uncovered one of nature's best-kept secrets. In 2006, a diver named Ben Raines was talking to the owner of a dive shop about the best places to find different species of fish and other sea creatures. The owner told Ben about an amazing discovery made by a local fisherman off the coast of Alabama in the Gulf of Mexico shortly after Katrina passed through. The owner had explored the area himself and told Raines that the site was an underwater cypress forest that served as a reef for wildlife.

However, he did not give Raines the exact location of the trees until 2012. Even then, the dive shop owner made Raines promise not to reveal the location to anyone. Raines became one of the first divers to explore the area that few people had seen for centuries.

The fifty-thousand-year-old underwater forest lies under sixty feet of water ten miles from the shore of Mobile, and the area covers about half a square mile. Raines said that the bald cypress trees were so well-preserved that cut samples of the wood smelled like sap. The forest was part of a primeval riverbed that ran through the area. His initial impression was that he had entered a fairy world. Several of the logs lying on the ocean floor were as large as trucks. Some of the stumps were between six and eight feet in diameter.

Scientists believed that the forest of cypress trees thrived for approximately 300,000 years. After the trees were submerged, they sank into the sediment and were preserved in the oxygen-free environment. Kristen DeLong, a researcher from Louisiana State University, said, "It [the wood] is a little bit darker in color than a piece of modern cypress, but if I didn't tell you it was over 50,000 years old, you would not know it." DeLong went on to say that, normally, trees that old would be approximately 120 feet under water. The fact that the trees were found in 60 feet of water indicates that the shoreline has risen about 60 to 100 feet. Because cypress trees can live to be 1,000 years old, the rings of these particular specimens can provide information about the climate history of the region.

III

BURIED SECRETS

HIDDEN CIVIL WAR GOLD

Tales of buried Confederate gold have spurred hundreds of treasure hunters in the Deep South for over a century. Most of these tales tell of gold that was hidden away to await the rise of the Confederacy or of gold that plantation owners buried to keep out of the hands of the invading Union army. Almost all of these legends can trace their origins to a historical footnote from New Orleans. On October 11, 1862, millions of dollars of Confederate gold were deposited at the Iron Bank in Columbus, Georgia. Just before the Union army attacked New Orleans, Confederate general P.G.T. Beauregard was sent to Columbus to transfer the gold from Young's bank. The fate of the Confederate gold remains a mystery, and various versions of the tale exist in Alabama.

In 1911, Jim Allen paid $1,000 for an eighty-acre plot of land that had been in the Robert C. Payne family in Rockville, Alabama, since 1850. In 1935, Jim Allen asked W.E. Woodson to look for gold on the site of an old smokehouse. Using a divining rod, Woodson walked through the area and concluded that there was no gold there. In the third week of January, Jim Allen's thirty-one-year-old son, Marshall, found a silver half-dollar from the nineteenth century in the same spot that Woodson had investigated during the third week of January. Marshall yelled to his younger brother, Claude, who began digging in the wet earth with a rake. According to an article published in the *Evergreen Courant* on January 28, 1937, the men made an amazing discovery within only twenty minutes:

> *They encountered a small porcelain urn, the top of which appeared to have been broken off recently. Inside were the glittering gold coins, their edges and contours as distinct as when they were minted, in 1861 or earlier, according to the dates thereon. While mostly in 20-dollar pieces, there were several five- and ten-dollar gold coins and a small amount of silver halves, quarters, dimes and half-dimes. The total face value of the find [was] approximately $2,700. Of this, $2,500 in gold and $5.65 in silver is being held in the Jackson, Ala. Bank & Trust Co.*

The Division of Coins allotted half of the find to Claude and the other half to Jim Allen. Marshall was reported to have complained, "It looks like I'm left out." The author of the article whimsically asserted that digging under old smokehouses had become a popular sport in Clarke County since the Allens' discovery.

A more apocryphal Civil War treasure story comes from Athens, Alabama. In the spring of 1865, Confederate soldiers were transporting two wooden crates by wagon across northern Alabama to the Confederate troops in Columbia, Tennessee. Inside the two-by-three-by-four-foot crates was $100,000 in gold and silver coins. As the wagon neared Athens, its wheels sank into the mud of a "bog hole." The soldiers were attempting to extricate the wagon from the mud when they received word that Union troops were on their way to Athens. Concerned that the two crates would fall into the hands of the Yankees, the soldiers hastily buried their cache of coins approximately a half mile west of an old stream. The general location lies four miles north of Athens. Legend has it that all of the soldiers who buried the coins were killed in battle before they could return to the burial site.

Nathan Bryan Whitfield was a prominent antebellum figure in Marengo County. One of the wealthiest men in the state, Whitfield moved to Marengo County in 1835 after he had purchased large tracts of land from George S. Gaines. By the 1850s, he had amassed a fortune estimated at $142,000. He completed his mansion, Gaineswood, in Demopolis in 1860. He and his wife, Elizabeth, had twelve children. He died in 1868.

One of the most enduring of the Whitfields' family stories was the tale of buried gold. During the Civil War, according to an article published in the *Evening Independent* on June 1, 1926, one of Nathan Bryan Whitfield's descendants, Gayus Whitfield of Middleboro, Kentucky, hired thirty black men to find a cache of gold coins buried somewhere on Shady Grove Farm. The gold was said to have been buried by Nathan Bryan Whitfield during the Civil War to keep it out of the hands of the invading Union army, just as many other wealthy planters had done. The farm was located near Jefferson, eighteen miles from Demopolis. For years, people had been finding loose coins on the property, so Gayus was pretty sure that there was even more gold just waiting to be found. Using an old map he had found amongst the papers of his father, C. Boaz Whitfield, Gayus instructed the men to look for an old boundary marker under which the gold was supposedly hidden. Apparently, Nathan Bryan Whitfield had drawn up a map of the exact location of the cache of gold years before and had given it to one of his four sons. The men looked for the marker for five days before finding it on May 31, 1926. At the base of the marker was an old, rusted powder can containing twenty-dollar gold pieces dated 1850 or earlier. The hoard was valued at over $200,000. Many local residents believe that even more coins are buried elsewhere on the land.

Another hoard of Civil War–era gold is said to be buried on the old Clements planation on the banks of Big Sandy Creek about twelve miles east of Tuscaloosa. Hardy Clements was a farmer, slave owner and politician who rode into Tuscaloosa in 1845 on a mule from Sumter County, South Carolina. At the time, he had only $100. Five years later, he had expanded his little farm to over nine thousand acres with holdings that included 113 sheep, 29 cows and 14 oxen. He was considered to be a very wealthy man by his contemporaries. Just before Brigadier General James H. Wilson's raiders arrived in Tuscaloosa on April 4, 1865, Clements decided to hide his gold for safekeeping. Supposedly, he buried his gold coins at night when everyone on the plantation was asleep so that he would be the only one who knew their exact location. Clements died in 1863 without telling anyone, not even his son, where the gold was. A number of possible locations have been suggested for the gold, including a place around the cotton gin, under the house, in his hog farm and in the slave section of the Clements family cemetery. Most of the former planation is now public land.

Many treasure hunters believe that the site of the old Nunez Ferry Crossing on the Perdido River is another good place to look for hidden gold. Henry Nunez established his ferry in 1815, and it was an integral part of a road that Nunez helped construct from Blakeley, Alabama, to Pensacola, Florida. All passengers riding into Blakeley by stagecoach crossed the Perdido River at Nunez's crossing because it was the only crossing for several miles in any direction. This traffic eventually made Nunez a wealthy man. In 1840,

Nunez was elected to the Florida Legislature, and nine years later, President Zachary Taylor awarded Nunez a U.S. Land Grant giving him ownership of all the land around his ferry crossing. When he was around seventy years old, Nunez's relatively peaceful existence came to an abrupt end in 1861 when a gang of bandits rode up to his house. They had heard that Nunez had a hoard of gold hidden somewhere on his property, and they demanded that he tell them where it was. When Nunez refused, they put a rope around his neck and hauled him up into a tree. In another version of the tale, a company of Union soldiers demanded to know the location of Nunez's gold. They decided to "loosen his tongue" by stringing him up by his thumbs on an overhanging tree limb. To end her husband's suffering, Mrs. Nunez led the men to a rose bush where he had buried a large cache of gold coins. Nunez died not long thereafter from an infection and pneumonia as a result of the beating. The Nunez Ferry remained in operation until 1919, when it was replaced by a bridge on U.S. Highway 90. Today, many people believe that the old ferryboat man buried a smaller cache of gold coins somewhere on his land in the event that the larger cache was stolen.

FORT MORGAN'S MYSTERY SHIP

Hurricane Isaac was first detected in the Lesser Antilles on August 21, 2012. On August 27, the hurricane passed near the Florida Keys. On August 28, the storm was officially designated as a hurricane, and the next day, it made two landfalls in Louisiana. Hurricane Isaac continued on through Mississippi, Alabama and Arkansas before dissipating on September 1. Hurricane Isaac brought 11.29 inches of rain to Mobile. Severe flooding was reported in Mobile, Bayou la Batre, Gulf Shores and Orange Beach. For the most part, Hurricane Isaac's visit to the Deep South left death and destruction in its wake. However, at Fort Morgan, the hurricane also left behind a relic from Alabama's past.

After Hurricane Isaac made its way through southern Alabama, people began talking about a 150-foot-long, 30-foot-wide wooden ship that was uncovered on a private beach off Beach Boulevard about six miles from Fort Morgan. An old water pump, with a long pipe running down the center of the ship, was clearly visible. It turned out that several hurricanes— Camille (1969), Frederick (1979), Ivan (2004) and Ida (2009)—had partially uncovered the ship, but never to this extent. The more romantically inclined

Since 1969, hurricanes and tropical storms have uncovered the wreckage of a "mystery ship" on the beach about six miles from Fort Morgan. *Edibobb.*

residents believed the boat to be a Civil War blockade runner—either the *Ivanoe* or the *Monticello*—which was burned by the U.S. Navy in Mobile Bay. However, the *Monticello* was ruled out as a candidate because it was a sailing ship and the wreck was clearly steam-powered. Another possibility was a rumrunner called the *Aurora*, which was carrying a cargo of 1,400 cases of alcohol when it was apprehended by the U.S. Coast Guard cutter *Forward* at the mouth of the Mississippi River. The authorities ordered that the ship be towed to Mobile, but it caught fire and sank near Fort Morgan in 1933.

Eventually, a historian affiliated with the Fort Morgan Historical Society, Mike Bailey, positively identified the ship as the *Rachel*: a three-masted ship that was built in 1919 at the De Angelo and Sons Italian Shipyard in Moss Point, Mississippi. In 2008, Bailey told the *Mobile Press-Register* that it was one of the largest Biloxi schooners ever built. "It was built as a lumber schooner and was carrying a load of lumber when it ran into a storm [in 1923]," Bailey said. "It didn't have a full crew, and they couldn't handle the ship in the storm. They put out an anchor, but [the ship] ran aground." Bailey went on to say that Ken D'Angelo, the great-grandson of the owner of the D'Angelo shipyard, showed him documentation, photographs and the original building plans of the *Rachel*. Anecdotal evidence from people living in the area at the time the ship ran aground also identified the wreck as the *Rachel*. However, because the name of the ship does not appear on its hull, its identity will undoubtedly continue to be contested the next time wind blows the sand away from its resting place.

"THERE'S A DINOSAUR IN MY FRONT YARD!"

In 1986, the State Highway Department made a discovery that placed a rural Alabama town in the national spotlight. Fifty miles southwest of Montgomery in Lowndes County, a road crew was excavating fill dirt for a highway nearby when it uncovered the bones of what appeared to be a prehistoric creature. Homeowner Catherine Hollingshead notified University of Alabama geology professor Douglas Jones of the find. "I wanted to tell everyone they found bones seventy thousand years old right out in front of the house, but I had to keep it a secret for ten days," she said. When Dr. Jones arrived, he and his associate told her that she had misunderstood when they told her the age of the fossils. They said, "Mrs. Hollingshead, that's seventy million years old!" The two men closely examined the six-foot skull and jaw cropping out of the ground at the bottom of the excavation site. The bones, which weighed about ten thousand pounds, turned out to be the remains of a *Mosasaur*.

Mosasaurs were a family of aquatic lizards that swam in the Cretaceous sea between 100 and 66 million years ago. The name *Mosasaur* is Latin for "Meuse lizard," and they were given this name after the first *Mosasaur* fossils were found in a quarry in Maastrict on the Meuse River in the Netherlands. *Mosasaurs* consist of six sub-families. Even though *Mosasaurs* have been found all over the world, most of the finds have been made in North America. Because of their hinged jaws, they were able to swallow prey of different shapes. Naturalist Robert W. Gibbs uncovered the first *Mosasaur* fossils in Alabama in the Mooreville Chalk formation in Lowndes County between 1850 and 1851. The nearly intact post-cranial skeleton of the species *Clidastes propython* was found by Edward R. Showalter near Uniontown in 1869. This is the most common species native to Alabama, although at least ten other distinct species of *Mosasaur* fossils have been discovered in the state. *Mosasaur* specimens are on display at Auburn

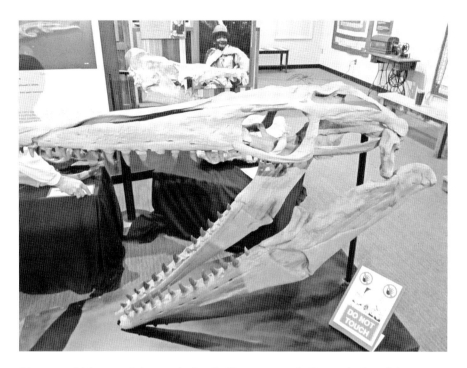

Mosasaurs, which roamed the seas during the Cretaceous period, were the last of the great marine reptiles and reached lengths of over fifty feet. *Alan Brown.*

University's Museum of Natural History, Birmingham's McWane Science Center and the Alabama Museum of Natural History. Professor Bethany Latham, from Jacksonville State University, said she would not be at all surprised if new species of *Mosasaurs* are found in Alabama and elsewhere in the future.

ALABAMA'S BURIED GIANTS

Tales of a forgotten race of giants have been embedded in American folklore for centuries. In 1541, Fernando de Soto's troops were marching from the Florida Panhandle to central Georgia when they encountered members of the Okonee and Tamatli tribes who towered over the Spanish by at least a foot. Their height earned them the name *Los Indios Gigantes*—the Gigantic Indians. While building Fort Loudoun in Winchester, Virginia, in 1754, the construction crew under George Washington's command discovered a cemetery of seven-foot-tall skeletons. In his book *The Ancient Giants Who Ruled America*, Richard Dewhurst recounted the discovery of the bones of giants in the nineteenth and twentieth centuries. For example, in 1871, two hundred skeletons ranging in height from seven to nine feet were uncovered from a mound on the banks of the Grand River in Cayuga, New York. In 1883, a group of archaeologists led by Colonel Morris of the Smithsonian Institute was excavating a mound in Charleston, South Carolina, when it discovered a giant skeleton surrounded by a circle of ten smaller skeletons.

That same year, in Wheeling, West Virginia, a cluster of giants, all about seven feet tall with low foreheads, was discovered in a mound. In 1888, a military contingent called the Logan Greys raised up a flat stone and discovered a deep hole at Eagle Lake, near Warsaw in Kosciusko County, Indiana. While exploring the hole, the men found an entrance to a twenty-five-foot-deep cave containing the skeletons of a six-foot-nine-inch giant buried beside a sacred pool. In 1912, a gigantic jaw bone with double rows of teeth was uncovered in Jennings County, Indiana. In the late nineteenth century, Alabama joined the ranks of states in which evidence of giant Native Americans has been uncovered.

During the first days of April 1886, Georgia, Alabama and Tennessee were buffeted with torrential downpours. The record rainfall of seven to twelve inches produced heavy flooding. In Alabama, the Coosa River rose six feet higher than normal. The river was so high in Gadsden, in fact, that a riverboat docked at the intersection of Fourth Street and Town Creek. A number of people had to be evacuated from the city's low-lying areas. Even though Etowah County's farmers and lumber operators were heavily impacted by the flooding, the total monetary loss amounted to only $100,000. Unexpectedly, the flood also uncovered a large number of Native American artifacts that had been lying underground for centuries. Most of the relics were uncovered on property owned by Colonel Sam Henry and Green Foster. Colonel Henry's farm was spread over 250 acres of fertile bottomland on the western banks of the Coosa River. When Colonel Henry's son, James R. Henry, began walking around the farm to assess the damage, he was dismayed to find that the flood had washed away the topsoil to a depth of about three to four feet, leaving only 40 to 50 acres of cultivatable land.

As Henry continued the investigation of his family's property, he discovered that the raging waters had exposed an unusual Native American burial site. The May 1, 1886 edition of the *Etowah County News* reported on Henry's amazing find:

Mr. James Henry, who discovered the bones of the big skeleton on his father's farm on the bank of the Coosa River near Gadsden, says that he could easily place his head in its skull and the bone was half an inch thick. The thigh bone was about twenty-two inches in length and three times as large as the bone in an ordinary man. The bone from the shoulder to elbow measured about twenty inches, and when all the bones were placed in their proper places, they showed that the owner, when alive, must have been at least twelve feet from the top of his head to the bottom of his feet. Two or three of these enormous skeletons were found.

For several weeks, the Henry family put the skeletons on display. No one knows where the skeletons are now. One could say that the fate of the Henry skeletons is as mysterious as their identity.

Alabama's Ancient Cave Coffins

When Revered William N. Crump moved to a farm outside Oneonta in 1840, he was like thousands of other settlers who moved to Blount County to make a permanent home for themselves. The 246-acre plot of land that the twenty-two-year-old pioneer purchased from the U.S. government contained entrances to five caves: Crump's Cave, Second Cave, Horseshoe Cave, Bishopella Cave and Sewer Cave. Crump and his hunting buddies stumbled upon what has come to be known as Crump's Cave in 1840. With a great deal of effort, the men squeezed through the narrow opening and found a treasure-trove of Native American artifacts, including spears and arrows, copper trinkets, stone axes and beads. They also discovered over two hundred pounds of galena, which is used in lead and silver. The hunters' most amazing find, however, was a collection of about eight to ten wooden boxes that appeared to have been hollowed out of logs with stone tools and fire, like dugout canoes. Crump left his farm during the Civil War to serve in the Forty-Ninth Alabama Infantry, but he returned after 1865.

In 1892, geologist Frank Burns visited Crump's Cave, which had been mined for saltpeter during the Civil War. In an account published by Burns that same year in the "Report of the U.S. National Museum," Crump wrote, "The coffins are about 7.5 feet long, 14 to 18 inches wide, and 2.5 inches thick and 6 or 7 inches deep." Burns said that after making the remarkable discovery, Crump and his friends returned to the cave on several occasions and removed an assortment of artifacts, including a human skull. Burns donated the deteriorating remains of the coffins to the National Museum, which was associated with the Smithsonian Institute. Ironically, the museum did not prove to be a good home for the priceless artifacts. In 1950, renowned author Fredrick J. Pohl wrote to a friend that the Smithsonian Institute had lost the coffins. To this day, the exact location of Crump's coffins is unknown.

Alabama's Lost Silver Mine

When one thinks of mining, the southwestern states usually come to mind. However, Alabama has a long history of mining. Gold fever made its way to Alabama following the discovery of gold in Georgia in 1828. Gold was first discovered in Alabama at Arbacoochee and Goldville in 1830. The discovery was made along Blue Creek and Chestnut Creek. However, gold has also been found in streams and creeks in Wedowee, Tallapoosa County, Cleburn County, Clay County and the Talladega National Forest. Gold production in Alabama amounted to approximately fifty thousand troy ounces up until World War II. Ironically, Alabama's most legendary mine is not a gold mine.

In the early 1830s, relations between Native Americans and white settlers were, for the most part, amicable. In 1832, measles raged through one of the small Native American villages. One of the settlers living nearby, Isaac Stone, rushed to the village as soon as he heard of the epidemic and treated as many of the villagers as he could. His actions saved an untold number of lives. One of the Native Americans whose life he saved, George, became a close friend of Stone's. In a letter included in *Historical Tales of Talladega*, Stone revealed that George "went into seclusion once or twice during each year," and that when the seclusion ended, all the Native Americans had new silver ornaments, armlets, beads and other pieces of jewelry. Stone supplied the Native Americans with whiskey to get them to tell him the location of the silver, but to no avail. In desperation, he enlisted the aid of several of his friends to help him find the silver mine. Stone deduced that the mine must be close to the village because the train of pack ponies always returned to the village loaded with silver ore within a short period of time. One day, after extracting the date of the tribe's next trip to the silver mine from George, Stone and his friends decided to follow the Native Americans. They traveled for several miles until the trail ended abruptly at Wolf Creek. The men split up and searched in opposite directions, but to no avail. Just before calling a halt to their endeavors, one of the men picked up a strange-looking rock, which turned out to be a four-pound rock of silver ore. In 1874, the rock was assayed at 70 percent silver and 30 percent lead.

The story of the men's discovery was soon leaked, which spurred a frantic hunt for the mine. No trace of the mine was ever found, aside from the rock that evidently fell out of one of the Indians' packs. Before the tribe was forcibly moved to Arkansas, the Native Americans are said to have buried their cache of silver in the vicinity of the mine.

THE LOST CANNONS OF FORT TOULOUSE

Fort Toulouse was strategically built near the confluence of the Coosa and the Tallapoosa Rivers in 1717. The French intended for the fort to become a deterrent to the encroaching British and Spanish armies and to serve as a trading post with the Creek tribe of Native Americans. The fort was constructed of logs one foot in diameter and nine feet in length, encompassing approximately one hundred yards. The interior of the fort consisted of an armory, a moat, barracks, separate quarters for officers and enlisted men and a garden. A watchtower was added later on. Fort Toulouse was one of the French Empire's last forts to receive improved artillery, new guns and medical supplies. The cannons were probably made of logs nine feet long and one foot in diameter. Between fifteen and thirty men were stationed at the fort at one time. Because of the region's hot and humid climate, the logs rotted quickly, forcing the soldiers to rebuild parts of the fort in 1721 and between 1733 and 1736. By 1748, the fort was moved because the river's current was eroding its foundation. Fort Toulouse was rebuilt twice more in 1751 and in 1755. In 1756, the fort's contingent of soldiers was increased to fifty men. Ironically, Fort Toulouse never saw combat. The French abandoned the fort between 1763 and 1764. Before leaving, the French spiked the cannons and dumped them into the fort yard. Gunpowder was poured into the Coosa River. The remains of Fort Toulouse were soon obliterated by the encroachment of the forest. By the end of the eighteenth century, all that remained were a few cannons lying in the weeds.

Only two of Fort Toulouse's cannons have been found; one is on display in the Wetumpka Courthouse at Wetumpka, Alabama, and the other is on exhibit in the State Department of Archives and History in Montgomery. Archaeologists believed that the remaining six cannons are either lying in the muddy bottom of the Coosa River or are covered by layers of dirt and debris on the fort site. Their discovery would be an invaluable aid to understanding Alabama's colonial history.

BIRMINGHAM'S UNDERGROUND RIVER

Birmingham's earliest settlers learned of the existence of an underground river running across the full length of Jefferson County from the Native Americans. The river, which flowed north and surfaced as a spring at Fifth Avenue and Twenty-Second Street, proved to be a convenient source of drinking water for people living in the area until it dried up in the twentieth century. In the 1880s and 1890s, offices in the vicinity of Fifth Avenue and Twenty-Second Street sold tickets to the "Mystic Underground River." Ticket buyers riding in small boats took guided excursions down the river.

The entrance to the river was sealed in the early 1900s because too many young people were making their way down to the river.

However, the downside of living on top of an underground river became a reality in the late nineteenth century when the city's building boom began. A newspaper article published in the *Birmingham Age* on May 7, 1886, reported a rumor that the city hall building was sinking: "It was discovered in the office of the city clerk and treasurer that the floor had sunk three inches in one place, and that near the front door the iron foot-plates were gradually sinking." The reporter added that the big spring on the south side had "no bottom" and that a mud hole that never dried up had formed in front of the school building.

The underground river made its presence known again in the twentieth century. Architects soon discovered that the city's spongy limestone subsurface sometimes made construction projects complicated. During the construction of the Tutwiler Hotel in 1913, workers had to build bridge-like crisscross beams across the ceiling of the river. An attempt was made that same year to build a luxury hotel that would rival the Tutwiler, but the basement was

To prevent the Tutwiler Hotel from crashing through the ceiling of Birmingham's underground river, workmen constructed a foundation of iron beams. *Alan Brown.*

During the construction of the Birmingham Public Library in 1982, one of the immense columns disappeared into a hole in the ceiling of the underground river. *Alan Brown.*

limited to one story instead of two stories, similar to the Twentieth Street Hotel. Construction of the hotel, called the Rhoden, was never completed because of the steel shortages during World War I. Eventually, the building's steel girders were dismantled and sold to support the war effort. In the 1920s, the construction company downsized the projected ten-story Florentine Club to two stories because of the weak foundation. When the Daniel Building was being constructed on Twentieth Street just south of the L&N Railroad tracks, builders had difficulty finding a solid rock for its foundation. Sump pumps were installed to keep the floor dry, and while an annex was being built for the Federal Reserve Bank at Fifth Avenue and Eighteenth Street North, water had to be pumped out of the foundation. On the plus side, a number of buildings constructed along the underground river sunk wells into it for heating and air conditioning.

The underground river was still creating problems for builders in the 1980s. Hope Cooper, a librarian, had vivid memories of the obstacles the river created during construction of the Birmingham Public Library in 1982:

This happened in October [or] *November 1982. We broke ground in June 1982. When they dug the first column, they hit a cistern from an old house that used to be there. That didn't present any problems.* [Then they began work on the second column.] *They dug the hole, put the rebar in, poured the concrete, and capped it off. When they came back the next morning, the column was gone. That's my memory of it at the time. I talked to my boss, George, and he said, "I remember that they kept pouring the concrete in, and it wouldn't fill up." What they ended up doing was to dig a very, very large hole and put a very, very big pad under it so that the pressure would be spread out instead of going down to the bedrock, which wasn't there. I've got pictures of the hole and the pad* [that was put into place].

The underground river even interfered with the building of Interstate 20, which had to be rerouted because of the sinkholes. Some of these sinkholes are still visible along Interstate 20 West.

ALABAMA'S LOST PIRATE TREASURE

Stories of buried pirate gold have fueled the imaginations of generations of treasure hunters. Since 1795, people have been excavating Oak Island in Nova Scotia in search of treasure buried by pirates. Legend has it that pirates buried around 160 million pounds of gold on Cocos Island in the Pacific in 1820. Actually, the only pirate who was ever reputed to have buried his loot was Captain Kidd, who was said to have buried some of his gold on Long Island. Alabamians have also been telling tales of buried pirate treasure for hundreds of years.

One pirate who supposedly deposited his gold in the sands of Alabama's beaches was a legendary—and probably fictional—pirate named Jose Gaspar, also known as Gasparilla. Most of what is known of Gasparilla comes from John Gomez, a hunting and fishing guide and boat pilot who lived with his wife in a shack on Panther Key near Marco Island. Gomez, who was known to elaborate the many stories he spun, said that Gasparilla was born in Spain in 1796 and moved to Spanish Florida around 1783 to set up his base of operations on Gasparilla Island. According to Gomez, Gasparilla plundered treasure-laden ships in the Spanish Main and the Gulf of Mexico. Before his death in 1821, he is said to have accumulated a huge cache of gold. The story goes that Gasparilla entrusted ten of his men to bury twenty large chests full of gold and jewels, valued at $30 million today. Although most treasure hunters have focused their search in Florida, some people believe that Gasparilla buried several chests in different parts of Mobile Bay. However, because Gasparilla is most likely apocryphal, his gold probably is too.

The other pirate who is said to have buried treasure in Alabama is a real historical figure. Born in either Bordeaux or one of the surrounding French territories of Saint-Domingue around 1780, Jean Lafitte and his brother sold smuggled goods from a warehouse in New Orleans. By 1810, the Lafittes had moved to Barataria Bay, Louisiana, where they supplemented their smuggling operation with piracy. During the Battle of New Orleans in 1814, many of Lafitte's men joined the New Orleans militia or served as sailors. A number of Lafitte's men formed three artillery companies. However, his privateering had angered Louisiana governor William C.C. Claiborne, who offered a bounty of $500 for Lafitte's head. In 1817, Lafitte

The Gasparilla Pirate Festival, held almost every year in Tampa, Florida, since 1904, celebrates the exploits of Jose Gaspar, who was reputed to have buried gold in Florida and Alabama. *Wikimedia Commons.*

fled from Barataria Bay to Galveston, Texas. Lafitte was killed in 1823 near Honduras during a sea battle with two heavily armed Spanish pirate ships. Not long after Lafitte's death, rumors began spreading about his loot, which he was said to have buried near Galveston and somewhere along coastal Louisiana around Lake Charles and Contraband Bayou. Some say that he also buried $80,000 in gold coins on a beach in Bayou La Batre near Mobile. Others believe that he buried some of his $10 million worth of plunder near Fort Morgan.

IV
MYSTERIES FROM THE SKIES

THE ODYSSEY OF EASTERN AIRLINES FLIGHT 576

One of the first major UFO sightings after World War II took place over Alabama on July 23, 1948. Captain Clarence S. Chiles and his co-pilot, John B. Whitehead, were piloting a DC-3 passenger plane from Houston, Texas, to Boston, Massachusetts. Both men were seasoned pilots who had served in the U.S. Air Force during World War II. At 2:45 a.m., the plane was about twenty miles west of Montgomery, Alabama, when Chiles and Whitehead saw a large object flying directly toward them. Later, Chiles told authorities, "It was heading southwest, exactly opposite to our course. It flashed down toward us at terrific speed. We veered to the left, and it passed us about seven hundred feet high." Whitehead described the UFO as being cigar-shaped, approximately thirty yards long and twice as wide as a DC-3. The pilots also noted that the object was wingless, that it had two rows of glowing windows and that it glowed with a dark blue light running along the fuselage. A projection resembling a radar aerial jutted from the nose of the craft. The object's flaming tail was ten to fifteen yards long. The flame's color was a dark orange in the center and a lighter orange along the side.

The UFO was no more than a few dozen yards away when it pulled up with a violent jerk and soared up in the air at a right angle. Within a few seconds, it was gone. Chiles and Whitehead surmised that the pilot of the UFO abruptly changed course after catching sight of the DC-3. The object

Developed by the Douglas Aircraft Company in 1935, the DC-3 made commercial aviation possible. *MKFI.*

was so close to the DC-3 that the plane rocked violently in its wake. The pilots estimated that the object was flying at a speed of five hundred to seven hundred miles per hour up to the moment it sharply maneuvered to avoid collision. The entire incident lasted only a few seconds, but it seemed much longer. Eager to find out the responses from the passengers, Chiles walked into the passenger cabin. Because it was 3:00 a.m., everyone was asleep except for the assistant managing editor of the *American Education Press* in Columbus, Ohio, Clarence McKelvie. Chiles and Whitehead breathed a sigh of relief when McKelvie substantiated their story: "I saw no shape or form. It was on the right side of the plane, and suddenly, I saw this strange, eerie streak out of my window. It was very intense, not like lightning or anything I had ever seen." In an interview with the Associated Press, McKelvie admitted that the UFO had flown too fast for him to give a detailed description of it.

The U.S. Air Force investigated the incident over the next few weeks. The investigators concluded that the object did not match any other aircraft in the area. They did not speculate as to the origin of the unidentified flying object.

THE FALKVILLE ALIEN

One of the strangest UFO sightings in the United States occurred on October 17, 1973, in Falkville, Alabama. Police Chief Jeff Greenhaw was sitting at home at 10:00 p.m. when he received a phone call from a woman claiming to have seen a strange object with flashing lights land in a field just west of town. The fact that several UFOs had recently been sighted in South Morgan County compelled Greenhaw to bring along his Polaroid camera just in case there was some truth to the woman's story. Greenhaw said he was driving to the remote area in his squad car when a weird figure suddenly appeared in the middle of the road. Afterward, Greenhaw told reporters, "I got out of the car and said, 'Howdy, stranger.' He didn't say a word, so I reached back, picked up my camera, and started taking pictures of him." Greenhaw took four departing shots of the creature before climbing back in the car and turning on his blue flashers.

The frightened alien then took off running. "I jumped in my car and took after him, but I couldn't catch up with him. He ran faster than any human I ever saw." Greenhaw described the stride of the "spaceman" as being extraordinarily long and robot-like.

Sheriff Greenhaw's life spiraled out of control following his interview on NBC-TV news. Not only did he begin receiving threatening phone calls in the two weeks following his interview, but his wife left him, his car's engine exploded and all of his possessions were destroyed in a fire that gutted his trailer, including his original photograph of the humanoid creature clothed in a silver space suit. Eventually, the negative publicity cost Greenhaw his job as sheriff. If Greenhaw did fabricate his sighting, as some people believe, he paid a hefty price for his deception.

THE FYFFE, ALABAMA SIGHTING

On February 11, 1989, the Fyffe Police Department received a telephone call from a woman claiming to have seen a strange object in the sky. The police continued receiving eyewitness reports throughout the night and the next day. By 11:59 p.m. on February 12, over fifty people had phoned in their sightings to the police. One of the witnesses described the object as "hovering at an angle from one o'clock to seven o'clock with bright lights at the top and bottom. The curvature was outlined in green with a bright light in the center." Their curiosity aroused, the police chief, Charles "Junior" Garmany, and his assistant, Fred Works, were in their squad car on their way to the area of the first sighting when they saw a huge metallic object up in the sky. The UFO appeared to be triangular. "The object came on over and got straight overhead," Works told a reporter. "We kept waiting to hear the sound. We kept looking at each other and saying, 'Where's the sound?' We never heard anything." Other law enforcement officers, including the Geraldine police chief, a Crossville police officer and a state trooper, had their own sightings of the weird object.

Over the next few days, the media and curiosity-seekers descended on little Fyffe, Alabama. Over one hundred newspapers, radio stations and television stations dispatched reporters to Fyffe. Once word of the sightings became widely known, more than four thousand tourists visited Fyffe. Because one of the eyewitnesses had described the UFO as being banana-shaped, one enterprising individual began selling T-shirts emblazoned with a drawing of a banana-shaped spaceship. The caption underneath read, "I survived the Fyffe UFO." Before long, Fyffe's overnight notoriety became tiresome. In an article appearing in the *Tuscaloosa News* on February 17, 1989, Chief Word was quoted as saying, "I walked into the grill the other day for lunch, and there sat a reporter. I never even got to eat. I came on back to the office, and there sat reporters from a TV station...Right now, I'm two wreck reports behind."

Ironically, the gawkers and jokes became tolerable after the citizens of Fyffe realized the possible economic windfall of their newfound fame. Soon, Fyffe began holding its own UFO Festival in

August. Thousands of tourists flocked to Fyffe's celebration, lured by its arts and crafts displays, games, hot air balloons, street dances and musical entertainment. The strange events of February 11 and 12, 1989, have found a unique place in the little town's history and in the annals of UFO sightings.

Fortean Evidence from Alabama

Charles Fort was one of the pioneers in UFO research. Born in Albany, New York, on August 9, 1874, Fort seemed to go out of his way to be different. Almost six feet tall, Fort sported a bushy moustache and thick-lensed glasses due to his failing eyesight. Fort was a very bookish, introverted man who had no friends, except for the writer Theodore Dreiser. Fort started out writing novels, but after writing 3.5 million words, he burned his manuscripts and notes, much to Dreiser's dismay, because he had not written what he wanted. Fort then decided to start his career as an "ultra-scientific realist." He devoted the next eight years to researching the unexplained in obscure books and newspaper articles. He was attempting to find the widest range of data related to strange events so that he could formulate a type of cosmic law. Fort estimated that by the time he had completed his research, he had written over forty thousand notes, which he collected in a volume titled *The Book of the Damned* (1919).

Fort used the word "damned" in the title to refer to data that scientists excluded as being inconsequential. *The Book of the Damned* is a fascinating early look at strange occurrences that defy explanation, such as blood rain, frogs, fish and chunks of meat that fall from the sky, lost planets and triangular clouds. He also described flying cylinder-like objects in the sky that appear to be precursors of today's UFOs. A number of these otherworldly visitations took place in the Deep South in 1896. Fort reports that during the summer of that year, hundreds of dead birds, including woodpeckers, wild ducks, cat birds and a number of canary-like birds, fell from the sky in Florida and Louisiana. Fort speculated that because hundreds of birds had fallen to the ground on a clear day, it stood to reason that even heavier objects could have fallen in Alabama. Fort went to his grave in 1932 without explaining what these "large objects" were that fell from the Alabama skies. However, he does suggest that alien visitors to our planet may have been responsible:

My own notion is that, in the summer of 1896, something, or some beings, came as near to this earth as they could, upon a hunting expedition; that in the summer of 1896, an expedition of super-scientists passed over this earth, and let down a dragnet—and what would it catch, sweeping through the air, supposing it to have reached not quite to this earth.

No evidence has ever surfaced to support Fort's theory; however, one year later, the citizens of Aurora, Texas, reported that a spaceship crashed into Proctor's windmill. A coincidence?

"IT CAME OUT OF THE SKY—IN SUMTER COUNTY, ALABAMA"

In 2002, Mike Morgan was a non-traditional student enrolled at the University of West Alabama. At the time, Mike was a retired member of the U.S. Navy who was working on his master's degree in English while teaching at Sumter Academy, a private school in Sumter County. During the spring semester, he was enrolled in my night class, "Teaching Composition." One night after class, he and I were talking about unexplained phenomena, and he mentioned a UFO sighting he had had two semesters before:

I was driving home late at night from one of Dr. Joe Wilkins's history classes on Highway 11 from Livingston to my home in York. I was thinking about the class I had just left. [As I passed] a stand of pines [that are] on the left as you are leaving Livingston, I looked up in the sky, and I saw what looked like a low-altitude aircraft. It seemed to be on fire. I was sure it was going to crash. When I got home, I went next door to see my neighbor, Stan Boutwell. He is a deputy sheriff here in Sumter County. I said, "Stan, would you like to go out with me and look for an aircraft that just went down?" He said, "Yeah." He called it in [to the sheriff's office]; I called NAS Meridian and informed the navy personnel out there that one of their aircraft went down.

We went out to the woods and looked for signs of flames and smoke. We didn't find anything, so we went to the York Airport [to look] for signs of anything that had crashed there. Later, Stan told me that the Navy claimed that it was a meteor that had landed in the Gulf of Mexico. The flying object looked like a yellow and bluish ball. It didn't look like a laser light or anything like that. It appeared to be flying fairly slowly. There was no noise from it. I watched it go out of sight. I'm retired navy—senior chief petty officer—and I've been on two aircraft carriers. At first, I was convinced that it was an aircraft. Now, I'm not so sure.

I then drove to the York Police Department [to report what I had seen]. There was a car in front of me that was slowing down. They were about fifty feet ahead of me. I thought they were on their cell phone. The car pulled into the police department's parking lot. One of the people was a lady—she was the pastor of a church in Livingston. She was with a member of her congregation—a very large fellow. They had seen it too.

[A few days later], I spoke to Dr. Pittman [a history professor at UWA] about the sighting. He agreed with the navy that it was probably a meteor. He said, "Your depth perception of the thing was off because you had nothing to bounce it off of." He was right. There was nothing in the sky to get a sense of depth perception. Still, Dr. Pittman is known to be pretty skeptical about some things.

I was convinced that I had seen it, and a bit embarrassed. Stan said that they kind of picked at him a bit the following day about seeing the UFO.

Ann Hodges: Alabama's Only Meteorite Victim

In November 1954, Sylacauga native Ann Hodges was taking a nap when a large rock crashed through the roof of her house, struck her radio and hit her on her side. Once she recovered her senses, Hodges discovered that she had a large, pineapple-shaped bruise on her thigh. The rock, which was twelve inches in circumference, was still warm to the touch. It turned out to be an eight-and-a-half-pound meteorite. She learned from her neighbors that they had seen a bright reddish light streak across the sky. Some believed that a plane had crashed in their little town; others, who were infected with Cold War paranoia, were certain that the Soviets were somehow responsible.

Word of the woman's bizarre encounter with a fiery visitor from outer space soon spread like wildfire. To Hodges, it seemed as if the entire town had flocked to her house to see her enormous bruise firsthand. News outlets from all over the country converged on Sylacauga in the hope of having an interview with the only person in history to have been hit by a meteorite in Alabama.

Ann Hodges became nationally famous almost overnight. However, before she could cash in on her newly found fame, the military confiscated the meteorite. Authorities feared that the strange object was a fragment of a Soviet satellite or even a state-of-the-art weapon. A few months later, the military determined that the rock was not of Soviet origin. However, before it could be returned to Ann and her husband Eugene, their landlord, Birdie Guy, sued Ann for ownership of the meteorite because it had landed on his property. A few weeks later, the Hodgeses bought the meteorite from Guy for $500.

Not long after settling out of court with Guy, Ann and Eugene Hodges received an offer from the Smithsonian Institute to purchase the meteorite. Convinced that they could make more money somewhere else, the couple turned down the Smithsonian's offer. However, by this time, the meteorite frenzy had died down, and no one was interested in paying top dollar for the meteorite. The Hodgeses ended up donating the meteorite to the Alabama Museum of Natural History, where it can be seen today.

The stress of dealing with the carnival-like furor over the meteorite, the military and their landlord took a heavy toll on Ann and Eugene Hodges. Ann eventually suffered a nervous breakdown, and in 1972, she and her husband divorced. Ann Hodges died of kidney failure in a nursing home without having made a cent on her meteorite.

V
PROPHETS AND SEERS

RENA TEEL: THE SEER OF MILLERVILLE

Rena Teel was born on April 8, 1894, near Rockford, Alabama. Her parents, James and Mary Smith Vansandt, were uneducated, and circumstances beyond her control forced Rena to drop out of school at age fourteen.

According to local legends, Rena was born with a caul covering her face, a sign that she was blessed with psychic insights. Her psychic abilities manifested themselves when she was very young. She exhibited an uncanny ability to inform her parents of where to find newborn calves or foals right after they were born. At age twelve, Rena predicted the death of her infant brother, George. Because the child was perfectly healthy, her mother ignored her warnings. For three days, Rena conveyed her concerns about her baby brother to her mother. On the fourth day, little George died, which convinced Rena's parents that she really did possess special powers. However, Mr. Vansandt downplayed Rena's abilities for fear that his family would be ostracized. As a preteen, Rena asked a local physician, Dr. M.J. Slaughter, what was wrong with her. All he could tell her with certainty was that she had a "sixth sense."

During her teenage years, Rena tried to conceal her gift because she did not want to draw attention to herself. As she grew up, though, Rena became more comfortable with the fact that she was different. After marrying Marvin Teel at age eighteen, Rena learned how to profit from her psychic abilities. When she and her new husband moved to Millerville, Rena began performing psychic readings for donations, usually fifty cents. Visitors waited for their turn to see Rena on her big front porch. Before long, word of her extraordinary gift spread through the community, even though she never advertised or posted a sign in front of her house. Her daughter, Dollie, recalled occasions when her family's yard was filled with cars. According to Rena's biographer, Ammie Anderson, her clientele included everyone from bootleggers and ex-convicts to industrialists, business leaders, congressmen and bank presidents.

One of the stories people told about her originated in Salem, where the Teels lived before moving to Millerville. One day, she warned her neighbor that his son would murder his cousin. At the time, the neighbor was renting a house to his nephew. Concerned for his nephew's welfare, he sent his son away to Florida hoping to invalidate the prophecy.

On another occasion, Rena was driving through Talladega when she noticed a scaffold erected in the center of town. She immediately told a friend of hers who lived in Talladega that they had to convince the judge that the man he had condemned to die was innocent. He had been charged with the crime of rape, and the girl he was accused of assaulting identified him as the culprit. Rena told her friend that the execution had to be stopped because the man was innocent. However, she refused to go to the judge because she feared retaliation from the victim's family. Two years after the man was executed, his uncle confessed the crime on his death bed.

Rena soon became known locally for her ability to find lost things—including people. John M. Williams said that his uncle asked Rena to help him find his missing billfold. She told him, "The man who took it is dishonest—you won't get it back." And he didn't. She seemed to specialize in aiding the authorities to find the bodies of people who had drowned. John M. Williams's cousin told him about a boy who had disappeared while fishing. Rena told the search party that the boy had drowned, and his corpse could be found in a specific location. She was correct.

Rena's most famous case took place on a cold February morning in 1949, when two-year-old Ricky Tankersley followed his father's hunting dogs into the woods. When he realized that his son was missing, L.C. Tankersley went to Rena, who told him where the child could be found. Tankersley followed her directions but was unable to find the little boy. He returned to Rena, who told him that he hadn't gone far enough. The man rushed back to the general area where Rena said the boy was lying on the ground. Tankersley had not gone very far from where he had originally stopped his search when he heard the dogs barking. He ran a couple hundred yards and was delighted to find that the dogs had slept on top of the little boy. The warmth they provided undoubtedly saved his life.

Rena's daughter Dollie told John M. Williams that her mother was a God-fearing woman who believed that God imbued her with her powers so that she could help others. When she died in 1964, Rena was known far and wide as the "seer of Millerville." For many years, people flocked to Millerville to view her house and seek out people who knew her.

Reverend Constantine Sanders: The Sleeping Preacher of Mooresville, Alabama

Constantine Sanders was born in 1831 in Madison County to James and Rebecca Sanders. The seventh of ten children, Constantine was, to all appearances, a perfectly normal child. At the age of twelve, Constantine decided that he wanted to devote his life to spreading the word of God as a preacher. However, in 1854, something happened that completely changed his life. He was boarding with Mrs. A.M. Harlow's family in Giles County, Tennessee, while attending seminary school in Elkton when he contracted typhoid fever. While in the throes of the disease, he began having convulsions. He told Mrs. Harlow it felt as if his skull had opened up:

Taking my hand with his, he placed it on his head, when, to my astonishment, I found what appeared to be a separation of the bone, nearly wide enough to bury my little finger, ranging from above his eyes near the center of his forehead to the top of his head. This condition of his head I saw frequently. When the paroxysms would subside, the opening would nearly close up.

Soon after his first convulsions, Constantine told Mrs. Harlow, "There will be a burying here before tomorrow evening [it being then in the afternoon], but it will not be any of your family." A few minutes after Constantine made his prediction, a man rode up from a community three miles away to see about burying someone in the family cemetery at the Harlow home.

Most of Constantine's early predictions centered on communities only a few miles away. Over the years, the range of his predictions extended

In the 1850s, the Reverend Constantine Blackmon Sanders, also known as the "Sleeping Preacher," was a pastor at the Mooresville Brick Church. *Alan Brown.*

considerably. When Constantine went into a trance, his eyelids fluttered and his chin drooped. Witnesses claimed that before he fell asleep, he made a grunting sound three times. He likened his psychic powers to having a head full of windows, which enabled him to view objects from any direction. Indeed, a number of people claimed that he had helped them locate lost or misplaced items.

Even though some people attacked him for his occult powers, Sanders viewed his abilities as being a gift from God: "My peculiar developments will not be explained from a scientific standpoint, at least so long as it is assumed my physical sufferings are the cause of my mental phenomena....I am a vessel of mercy whom the Lord hath chosen to this end."

In 1875, Reverend Sanders's notoriety spread when a reporter for the *Nashville Daily American* wrote an article about the minister's strange seizures. The writer referred to Sanders as "the sleeping preacher," a nickname that followed Sanders for the rest of his life. The seemingly endless stream of curiosity seekers in Mooresville made Reverend Sanders's life miserable. His suffering was alleviated somewhat when his friend, the Reverend G.

On top of the steeple of the Mooresville Brick Church is the Hand of God with the finger pointing upward, symbolizing the hope of heaven and the reward of the righteous. *Alan Brown.*

Washing Mitchell, wrote an authorized biography of Sanders in September 1876. The book, entitled $X+Y=Z$ or *The Sleeping Preacher of North Alabama*, was based on interviews with sixty-nine living witnesses, all of whom spoke of Reverend Sanders with deep respect.

On May 5, 1876, Reverend Sanders transcribed his final message from $X+Y=Z$:

> *My casket, I now come to address you personally before I depart. You have been to me a greatly submissive servant, in suffering, in contempt, in wonder, in reproach, by night and day from year to year past....I have given you many valuable lessons and prevented you from many difficulties and sorrows. With Heaven's benediction, I now bid you adieu.*

After twenty-two years, Reverend Sanders's psychic powers came to an abrupt end. For the next thirty-five years, Reverend Sanders suffered no more seizures. He passed away peacefully in 1911 at the age of eighty.

EDGAR CAYCE: SELMA'S SLEEPING PROPHET

Edgar Cayce, widely known as America's greatest prophet, was born on a farm near Beverly, Kentucky, on March 18, 1877. His parents, Leslie B. Cayce and Carrie Cayce, raised six children. At age ten, Edgar was taken to church, where he developed a lifelong love of the Bible. When he was twelve years old, Edgar discovered that he could learn his spelling words if he slept with his head lying on his spelling book. This ability did not surface again for several more years. In 1893, the Cayce family moved to Hopkinsville, Kentucky. Cayce did not attend high school because his parents could not afford to educate him beyond the eighth grade.

Cayce's psychic abilities became readily apparent in 1900 after forming a partnership with his father to sell Woodmen of the World Insurance. However, the Cayces' business abruptly ended after Edgar was struck by severe laryngitis. He was forced, by his infirmity, to stay at home with his parents and study photography, a trade that did not depend on his ability to speak. In 1901, Cayce became acquainted with a stage hypnotist named Al Lane, who attempted to cure Cayce's laryngitis through hypnotic therapy. Ten months later, Cayce's laryngitis appeared to be cured. Lane was astounded to discover that while under hypnosis, Cayce could discuss medical and scientific matters that someone with his level of education should have had no knowledge of. With Lane's encouragement, Cayce decided to offer trance healing to the general public. He was able to perform his healings with the person being present or through the knowledge of a person's name and location. Afterward, Cayce was unable to remember anything he had said during the readings. He diagnosed the physical or mental malady and then provided a remedy. Cayce received no money for his services.

Cayce's amazing powers soon became known throughout the region, thanks to the newspaper coverage his work received. In 1902, Cayce was hired by a bookshop in Bowling Green. He married Gertrude Evans on June 17, 1903. Gertrude's dislike of Cayce's readings aggravated his own concern over their morality. Cayce and a relative opened up two photographic studios in Bowling Green, but they burned down in fires in 1906 and 1907. Cayce was forced, by economic necessity, to take a job with the H.P. Tresslar photography firm. In October 1910, Dr. Wesley H. Ketchum from Hopkinsville persuaded Cayce to go into business with him.

In 1912, Cayce discovered that Ketchum had not been completely honest about the way the business was being run. That same year, Cayce worked at a photography studio in Selma, Alabama. Photographs bearing the Cayce studio mark can be found in homes throughout Selma. To help make ends meet, Cayce invented the card game Pit or Board of Trade. Cayce continued to give readings, but he had to ask for voluntary donations in order to support his family. While living in Selma, Cayce was approached by several businessmen who enlisted Cayce's aid in helping them make money by predicting the daily outcomes of the cotton market and local horse races. Cayce soon discovered that when he used his gift for monetary gain, he did no better than chance would allow. Consequently, Cayce decided to use his

Right: While living in Selma from 1912 to 1923, psychic Edgar Cayce operated a photography studio in this building. *Alan Brown.*

Below: In 1927, the Association of National Investigations built this hospital in Virginia Beach and dedicated it to the scientific study of Edgar Cayce's readings. *Gingerkrick.*

trance readings only to help people who were suffering. Most of the cures he suggested involved the use of ultraviolet light, gemstones, electrotherapy, massage and less work that was mentally taxing. Each year, hundreds of people traveled to Cayce's office to benefit from his miraculous healing powers. He insisted that the appointments be set up at either 11:00 a.m. or 3:00 p.m. on a specific day. During the 1920s, Cayce also became very interested in reincarnation. Sometimes, he would track his patients' lives back hundreds of years, linking them with the lost continent of Atlantis. However, Cayce continued to be concerned that his channeling sessions violated Biblical teachings.

In 1925, while in a trance, Cayce heard a voice that instructed him to move to Virginia Beach, Virginia. In this period of his life, Cayce worked as a professional psychic with a paid staff and volunteers. One of Cayce's admirers, a stock trader named Morton Blumenthal, built a house for Cayce and his wife in Virginia Beach. In 1927, the Association of National Investigations built a hospital in Virginia Beach dedicated to the scientific study of Cayce's readings. Cayce's fame spread even more following the publication of the first edition of his biography in March 1943. To meet the growing demand for his spiritual advice, Cayce had to increase the size of his office space. He became nationally famous following the publication of an article about him in *Coronet* magazine titled "Miracle Man of Virginia Beach." As the carnage of World War II increased, Cayce began to receive thousands of entreaties from grief-stricken families concerned about their loved ones who were missing in action. Soon, he increased the rate of his readings to eight per day, imperiling his health in the process. Cayce collapsed in August 1944, suffered a stroke in September 1944 and died on January 3, 1945.

Edgar Cayce was a very religious man who was plagued by fears that his work was not entirely Christian. The greatest insult, from Cayce's point of view, would have been to be called "un-Christian." Today, his work in the field is highly respected by thousands of scientists, theologians and experts in the paranormal. The accuracy of his predictions dumbfounded many of his skeptics when he predicted the discovery of Atlantis in the 1960s. In 1968, explorers diving near the Caribbean island of Bimini discovered undersea ruins and an ancient underwater road system that has come to be known as the "Bimini Road." Are these the remnants of the lost continent?

VI
NATIVE AMERICAN LEGENDS

THE LEGEND OF PRINCE MADOC

Ever since the arrival of the Europeans on the American mainland, explorers and colonists have spun tales of encounters with blue-eyed "white Indians" who spoke English. In 1666, Morgan Jones, the chaplain to the governor of Virginia, claimed to have narrowly escaped an attack from a band of white Native Americans who spoke English. Jones recognized the dialect as being similar to that spoken by his kinsmen in Wales. For generations, Cherokee tribes living in Alabama told tales of a white man whose ship arrived in Mobile hundreds of years ago.

In his book *Historie of Cambria* (1584), Humphrey Lloyd theorized that these "white Indians" were descendants of an expedition led by the Welsh prince, Madoc (sometimes spelled Madog) ab Owain Gynedd, and his brother, Rhiryd, in 1170. Madoc's ten ships sailed from the Afon Ganol in Penrhyn Bay to escape the feudal strife of their homeland. They were spurred on by Viking tales of a fabled land beyond the ocean. The ship arrived in Mobile Bay and headed west toward present-day Mississippi, Louisiana, Arkansas and Texas. The Welshmen also extended their explorations eastward, toward Georgia, and northward, toward North Carolina. Legend has it that the prince returned to Wales and persuaded others to join him on a second expedition to the New World. Madoc's ships sailed from Lundy Island in 1171 and were never heard from again.

In his book *History of Cambria* (1584), Humphrey Lloyd told the tale of Prince Madoc, who sailed from Wales to present-day Mobile, Alabama, in 1170. *William Cullen Bryant*, A Popular History of the United States.

In her article "A Consideration: Was America Discovered in 1170 by Prince Madoc Ab Owain Gwynedd of Wales?" author Jayne Warner asserts that the explorers left a series of forts along the route of the Alabama and Coosa Rivers where settlers would have arrived when entering Mobile Bay. All of these pre-Columbian forts were constructed in an architectural style unlike the Cherokee fortifications, which were primarily earthen structures. According to Judge John Haywood in his book *The Civil and Political History of Tennessee* (1823), five of these forts formed a circle around Chattanooga. The sixth fort, near DeSoto Falls in Mentone, bore a striking resemblance to Dolwyddelan Castle in Gwyneed, North Wales, which was the birthplace of Prince Madoc. The fort stood until the 1920s when it was dismantled by local residents who used the stones to construct roads and houses.

In the eighteenth century, the Mandan tribe living near Missouri was singled out by explorers and settlers as being the most likely descendants of Prince Madoc's expedition. Painter George was particularly taken by the women's white skin and their hazel, blue and grey eyes. He even claimed that the Mandans understood when addressed in the Welsh language. Unfortunately, the tribe was wiped out by a plague of smallpox in 1837, making it impossible to detect their Welsh ancestry using DNA. Still, enough evidence exists in support of Prince Madoc's expedition that the Daughters of the American Revolution placed a plaque alongside Mobile Bay in 1953. The plaque reads, "In memory of Prince Madog, a Welsh explorer who landed on the shores of Mobile Bay in 1170 and left behind, with the Indians, the Welsh language."

TECUMSEH AND THE NEW MADRID EARTHQUAKE

Shawnee war chief and political leader Tecumseh was born at Old Piqua in western Ohio in 1768. Growing up, he witnessed the border wars that ravaged the Ohio Valley. Following the death of his father, Puckeshinwa, at the Battle of Point Pleasant in 1774, Tecumseh was raised by an older sister, Tecumpease. In late 1789, Tecumseh and his brother conducted raids on small towns and villages in Tennessee and Kentucky. In 1794, he fought at Fort Recovery and Fallen Timbers. Undaunted by the Native Americans' defeat, Tecumseh did not participate in the signing of the Treaty of Greenville in 1795. Instead, he continued to wage war against the intrusion of the whites on Native American lands.

According to legend, Shawnee chief Tecumseh (1768–1813) caused the New Madrid Earthquake of 1811 or 1812 while trying to recruit Creeks from the south into his confederacy. *Deinocheirus.*

By the early 1800s, Tecumseh had become a mighty war chief. His powerful demeanor and charismatic personality contributed to his success, especially with young warriors located at a village in east-central Indiana. At the same time, Tecumseh's brother, Lalawethika, was also reaching a position of prominence as a result of his visions. Changing his name to Tenskwatawa or "The Open Door," he visited various tribes preaching a message of religious deliverance from the encroachment of white civilization. His accurate prediction of a solar eclipse on June 16, 1806, cemented his reputation as a religious leader. Thousands of Native Americans made the journey from their native lands in the Midwest to Tenskwatawa's Shawnee village in Greenville, Ohio.

The New Madrid Earthquakes, which began on December 16, 1811, and ended on February 7, 1812, caused ground warping, fissuring and landslides. The last earthquake created Reelfoot Lake in Lake County, Tennessee. *USGS-PD.*

Instead of opposing his brother, Tecumseh wisely decided to usurp his movement, converting it into a political juggernaut. Tecumseh and his brother, who is now known as the Prophet, relocated their settlement to the confluence of the Wabash and Tippecanoe Rivers. Under its new name, Prophetstown, the Prophet's new base of operation drew even more followers. Meanwhile, Tecumseh embarked on a mission to unite all of the Native American tribes on the continent in an effort to drive out the white man. He began his campaign in the Midwest after the loss of thousands of acres of Native American lands at the Treaty of Fort Wayne (1809). In November 1811, Prophetstown was completely destroyed by U.S. forces while Tecumseh was in the Southeast recruiting new members from the Alabama Creeks for his confederacy.

Upon his return to Michigan, Tecumseh was stunned to discover that Prophetstown had been burned by the American forces. For a while, he attempted to rebuild his shattered confederacy. Then during the War of 1812, he helped the British take Detroit and led a faction of pro-British Native American tribes against the Americans in southern Michigan and northern Ohio. Tecumseh joined the British in their retreat following Henry Harrison's invasion of northern Canada. Tecumseh died at the Battle of the Thames on October 5, 1813. His body was never recovered.

Tecumseh's most legendary act is said to have occurred in 1811 while he was traveling through the Southeast in order to recruit more Native Americans for his confederacy of Native American tribes. He addressed the chiefs of the Creeks, Seminoles, Cherokees, Chickasaws and Choctaws, and they all gave him their support. However, according to Elaine Hobson Miller, author of *Myths, Mysteries & Legends of Alabama*, he encountered some opposition when he arrived in the village of Tuckabatchee on the Tallapoosa River and laid out his plan to Big Warrior, chief of the Alabama Creeks. Big Warrior listened politely to Techumseh's speech. When Techumseh finished, Big Warrior informed him that his tribe was not interested in becoming part of his confederacy. Tecumseh flew into a rage and vowed that when he returned to his home, he would stamp his foot, the ground would shake, the rivers would flow backward, the sun would disappear into the darkness and Big Warrior's village would disappear. Tecumseh's dire prediction came true on December 16, 1811. People living in Kentucky, Tennessee, Indiana and Ohio were shocked to see the Mississippi River flow north temporarily and dust clouds obliterate the sun. Lakes appeared out of nowhere, and great fissures opened up in the ground. Countless trees and log cabins were laid waste. The epicenter of the earthquake, New Madrid, Missouri, was completely destroyed. Alabama was spared the destruction that many states experienced, with the exception of the village of Tuckabatchee, which was completely wiped out. Only the hut where Tecumseh spent the night remained in Big Warrior's village.

THE LEGEND OF CHEWACLA CREEK

Chewacla Creek is one of the two creeks that run through Chewacla State Park in Auburn, Alabama. Between the early 1840s and early 1900s, a sawmill owned by W.W. Wright operated on Chewacla Creek. The deep pool that was located around Wright's mill served as a popular swimming hole for many years. Following the purchase of the site by the federal government in

1935, the Civilian Conservation Corps (CCC) constructed six stone cottages on the property, as well as an arched masonry bridge, a bathhouse, two and a half miles of roads, two miles of foot trails and a concrete and stone dam. In 1939, the State of Alabama acquired the site and converted it into Chewacla State Park, which offers camping, boating, fishing and swimming. The area's rugged and natural beauty creates the perfect setting for the Creek Native American tale of an ill-fated romance.

Long before the first Europeans set foot in the American Southeast, a handsome young Creek brave named Chewacla became enamored with a beautiful Native American woman named Kiattina, who was from a neighboring tribe. Unfortunately, an enmity that sprung up between the two tribes doomed their budding romance from the start. The Creeks eventually relocated to Alabama, which made it difficult for the lovers to see each other again. In addition to the great mountain that separated the lovers, they were forbidden by their individual tribes to ever see each other again. Despite the obstacles that kept them apart, Chewacla's and Kiattina's love for each other burned even brighter.

The next spring, Kiattina wandered to the base of the mountain, lost in her dream of the halcyon days she had spent with Chewacla. At the same time, Chewacla also felt himself drawn to the mountain; he somehow sensed that Kitattina was standing on the other side. Suddenly, the couple were knocked to the ground by a rumbling deep under the ground. They stared in amazement as a huge pass was created inside the mountain.

Caution gave way to passion, and the lovers fell into each other's arms. Before they had a chance to even think about what had just happened to them, they heard the angry voices of her kinsmen from the north and his kinsmen from the south. Trapped inside the pass with no hope of escape, Kiattina and Chewacla agreed that death at their own hands was preferable to a lifetime of separation from each other. Chewacla drew his blade from its sheath and took Kiattina's life. He then stabbed himself and collapsed by her side.

For generations, Creek medicine men passed down the story of the couple whose love for each other was stronger than their fear of death. They said that a spell was cast on the spot where they had their last embrace. To this day, some people believe that couples who embrace here are eternally united, just as Kiattina and Chewacla were hundreds of years before. Others say that on still spring nights, one can hear the angry cries of their kinsmen. The legend's uncanny resemblance to Shakespeare's Romeo and Juliet can account for at least some of its durability.

THE LITTLE PEOPLE OF THE CHEROKEE

For hundreds of years, Cherokee tribes lived in the river valleys of northwest South Carolina, western North Carolina, eastern Tennessee and northern Georgia. The encroachment of white settlers in the late eighteenth century forced them to relocate to the west and the north. By 1782, many Cherokees had resettled in northeast Alabama. The Cherokee nation split during the Revolutionary War when a pro-British faction, the Chickamauga, moved farther down the Tennessee River and established the Five Lower Towns. In 1792, bands of Chickamauga from the Five Lower Towns began attacking neighboring white settlements. In 1794, they were defeated by militia leader James Ore, and by the early 1800s, thousands of Cherokees were living in northeast Alabama once again. Christian missionaries set up schools at Creek Path (1820) and White Town (1823). Many of them had been encouraged by the federally appointed land agent to give up hunting and take up farming and herding cattle. In 1813, the Cherokee sided with Andrew Jackson's forces in their fight against the Red Sticks, a warring faction of the Creeks. In 1814, during the Battle of Horseshoe Bend, the Cherokees created a rear diversion, allowing Jackson's forces to make a frontal assault and defeat the Red Sticks. The Cherokees' undeniable contribution to Jackson's victory did not insulate them from further land cessions in the Treaties of 1817 and 1819. The Cherokee lost all of their land in the Indian Removal Act of 1830, which resulted in their forced migration to Native American territory west of the Mississippi River.

Legend has it that the Little People accompanied the Cherokee during their forced evacuation from their homes in Georgia in 1838. While the Cherokee made the forced march to Oklahoma on the Trail of Tears in 1838, the Little People served as comforters and protectors. Before leaving, the Little People gave the Cherokee the gift

These Native Americans from the Cherokee Reservation in North Carolina are dressed in traditional Cherokee garb. *Boston Public Library.*

of eternal fire, which kept them warm in inclement weather. Some Cherokee believe that the eternal fire continues to burn to this day.

The Dogwood People have been known to steal children, but they are good; they tend to look out for human beings. The Laurel People are trickster figures who are vengeful and who have also been known to abduct children. They are fluent in both Cherokee and in their own language. The Little People are invisible most of the time, but they sometimes reveal themselves in the forest. People living close to their caves in the woods soon discovered that if they left food for them at night, the Little People would perform chores for them, like harvesting crops and plowing fields.

Some descendants of the Cherokee living in Alabama still tell stories about their encounters with the Little People. For example, in an interview with Garrett Pearson, David Saunooke described the Little People as "having their own personalities....They enjoy mischievous yet playful interactions with people." He went on to say that his grandmother met up with them several times: "One day, she lost her car keys and outright told the little people to 'quit messing with me.' She then found her keys [in] just moments." She insisted that despite their mischievous antics, many people view them as guardian angels.

THE LEGEND OF NOCCALULA FALLS

Noccalula Falls is a ninety-foot-tall waterfall located on land that was once owned by R.A. Mitchell, the former mayor of Gadsden, Alabama. In 1940, his daughter and heir, Sadie Mitchell Elmore, proposed to sell the land to the City of Gadsden for $50,000. Six years later, Gadsden purchased the land for $70,000 for the purpose of converting it into a state park. In the 1950s, the city began making improvements to the site, and in 1976, the park was listed in the Alabama Register of Landmarks and Heritage. Each year, over fifty thousand tourists are drawn to Noccalula Falls Park by the beauty and history of its aboriginal fort, caves, abandoned dam, Black Creek Gorge, Botanical Gardens, unusual rock formations, Civil War carvings, pioneer carvings, an old pump house for Dwight Cotton Mill and by the legend that gave the area its name.

According to the legend, Noccalula was the beautiful daughter of a Cherokee chief whose tribe lived near the falls. She was betrothed to the chief of a powerful rival tribe, but Noccalula was in love with a young man from her own tribe. Her father disapproved of the match because he was not nearly as wealthy as the young man he had chosen for her. She begged her father to allow her to marry her own true love, but he turned a deaf ear to her pleas. On the day of her wedding, Noccalula could not help but think of her beloved while her relatives clothed her in a beautiful dress. When no one was looking, she slipped away from the wedding party and rushed to the waterfall. The wedding guests stared in awe as Noccalula walked to the edge of the precipice and plunged into the churning waters below. Her guilt-

Noccalula Falls, a state park near Gadsden, Alabama, is the site of a legend about the illicit romance between a Cherokee princess and her true love. *Pixabay*.

stricken father decreed that the falls were to be known as Noccalula Falls from that day forward. For years, people venturing out to the falls on moonlit nights claim to have seen her ghostly form standing in the misty waters at the bottom of the falls.

The tragic legend of Noccalula provided the inspiration for one of the park's most prominent features. In the late 1960s, Suzanne Silvercruys was commissioned to create a statue of the doomed Cherokee princess. The project was funded by the Gadsden Women's Club and by local schoolchildren.

CHIEF TUSKALOOSA AND THE BLACK WARRIOR RIVER

Tuskaloosa, whose name means "Black Warrior," was the chief of a Mississippi band of Native Americans who lived in the present-day state of Alabama. The Choctaws and Creeks are, most likely, descendants of Tuskaloosa's tribe. He was said to be a giant man who was more than a foot taller than Hernando de Soto's invaders. Because of his height, Tuskaloosa was a very intimidating personage who was feared by his own people and by the neighboring tribes. In 1539, Hernando de Soto's exploratory force of six hundred to one thousand men and two hundred horses began making forays through modern-day Florida, Georgia, South Carolina and Alabama. In 1540, de Soto reached Tuskaloosa's Coosa Province and took its chief, Coosa, hostage. On September 18, 1540, he reached the town of Talisi. His men left the town on October 5 and made their way to the village of Atahachi. Tuskaloosa sat on a balcony on a platform mound wearing a headdress and a mantle of feathers. De Soto took Tuskaloosa hostage to assure safe passage.

Tuskaloosa led the Spaniards to a highly fortified village called Mabila. Tuskaloosa told de Soto that he wanted to stay in Mabila, but the Spaniard denied his request. After the chief of Mabila refused to furnish de Soto with porters, a fight ensued, during which the Mabilan chief's arm was cut off. Enraged, the Mabilans attacked the Spanish, who regrouped outside of the village and attacked it. After nine hours, the Spanish broke through the palisades and proceeded to burn down Mabila. Five thousand Mabilans were killed, including Tuskloosa and his son. De Soto lost twenty-two men. Even though de Soto won the Battle of Mabila, he lost so many horses and supplies that his campaign into Spanish Florida never recovered.

Today, Chief Tuskaloosa's name is memorialized in the city of Tuscaloosa and in the 178-mile Black Warrior River. Formed by the confluence of the Mulberry Fork and the Locust Fork of the Warrior River, the Black Warrior River flows through western Alabama into the Tombigbee River. It has an area of 6,275 square miles and a series of locks and dams that were built by the U.S. government in the 1880s to develop central Alabama's coal industries by making the river navigable along its entire course.

In her book *Alabama: One Big Front Porch*, Kathryn Tucker Windham tells the story of the centuries-old curse attached to the Black Warrior River. Shortly after being kidnapped, Tuskaloosa addressed his captors saying, "Cursed be the white man with his evil ways. Cursed be the white man who kills my people. The waters of our land will avenge the death of our warriors. The waters will consume our enemies. As long as the river flows, it will take the white man as a sacrifice." Windham goes on to say that in

The Black Warrior River in west-central Alabama flows for 178 miles to the Tombigbee River and passes through Tuscaloosa. *Alan Brown.*

the years following Tuskaloosa's death, at least one person has drowned in the Black Warrior River every year. Some Alabamians say that the body of a drowning victim can be found if a white shirt belonging to the person is thrown in the river. It will float directly over the spot where the body lies. For generations, white shirts floating down the Black Warrior River have been tragic reminders of the curse of Chief Tuskaloosa.

VII
LEGENDARY DEATHS

SPARTANA MORISETTE: THE LOST SOUTHERN BELLE

Some people are remembered more for the strange circumstances that surrounded their deaths than the quality of their lives. A good example is a tragic figure from Alabama's antebellum period named Spartana Morisette. She was the beautiful and gifted daughter of a prominent Alabama lawyer who was sent to Mobile by the Alabama legislature to institute reforms in the way cotton bales were sampled and inspected on the wharves. Spartana accompanied her father down the Alabama River in the hope of sampling some of the old port city's charms.

Unfortunately, Spartana's pleasure trip did not live up to her expectations. The strict new policies her father proposed were met with fierce resistance, according to an article published in the *Wilcox Banner* in Camden, Alabama, shortly after the Civil War:

> *A mob of cotton samplers, free negroes—called Creoles—and whites, congregated on the wharf to insult and, if necessary, to mob him, but with the aid of General Deshee and one or two other fearless friends with pistols in hand, he reached the hotel with his trembling young charge. Her anticipated pleasure was, of course, cut short, and over her protest—fearing a repetition of the scene recently enacted—she and her father took passage on the* New World *for their home.*

In the mid-nineteenth century, a young woman named Spartana Morisette disappeared from a steamboat similar to the one pictured here. *Library of Congress.*

Ironically, by attempting to save his daughter from possible bodily harm by booking passage on the *New World*, her father unwittingly set the stage for her untimely demise. After the steamboat landed, Spartana Morisette was found to be missing. The only traces she left behind were her footprints in the dew on the deck just aft of the wheelhouse. When an intensive search of the steamboat proved to be fruitless, a reward was offered for information regarding her disappearance and, hopefully, her present location. Dispatches were sent to steamboats paddling up the Alabama River from Mobile, instructing them to keep a coffin on board in the event that Spartana's corpse was found. After a few days, the girl's body was discovered by a steamer under the command of Captain Frank Johnson.

A number of explanations were offered for the girl's death. Foul play was the first possibility that came to mind. Some people believed that the rabble in Mobile was somehow responsible. However, one of the more widely accepted explanations was that Spartana was sleepwalking that fateful night and inadvertently stepped off the deck into the Alabama River. To this day, her death remains unsolved.

HARPER LEE AND THE VOODOO PREACHER OF ALEXANDER CITY

The Reverend Willie Maxwell was a charismatic African American minister who preached at several churches in Alexander City, Alabama, on the weekends. During the week, he supervised pulp wooding crews in a local pulp mill. Maxwell was also rumored to have connections with voodoo. Locals said that he was obsessed with the "Seven Sisters of New Orleans" who practiced voodoo in the 1920s.

In the 1960s and 1970s, he was implicated in a string of what at first appeared to be accidental deaths. On August 6, 1970, the *Alexander City Outlook* published a short article about Mary Lou Maxwell, whose lifeless body was discovered inside her 1968 Ford that appeared to have crashed into a tree. Her husband, Willie Maxwell, reported the accident at 2:45 a.m. Not long thereafter, Maxwell was indicted for the murder of his wife. He was acquitted, largely because of an alibi provided by his neighbor, Dorcus Anderson, and because of the expert defense provided by his attorney, former state senator Tom Radney. Aside from winning his freedom, Maxwell also collected $90,000 in insurance money.

Over the next several years, Maxwell's innocence was called into question following the deaths of people connected to him. In 1971, Maxwell's brother was found dead of alcohol poisoning, and some people believed that Maxwell had forced his brother to drink alcohol and embalming fluid. Three years later, Maxwell's second wife, his neighbor Dorcus Anderson, died. He had married her following the death of her husband. The coroner ruled that she had died of "acute asthmatic bronchitis," although she had a deep cut on her forehead at the time of her demise. Almost two years after her death, Maxwell collected $50,000 on her insurance policy. Then in 1976, Maxwell's nephew, James Hicks, was found dead in his car. Hicks had worked for Maxwell intermittently. No physical evidence connected Maxwell to his nephew's death. The "accidental death" that sealed Maxwell's fate occurred in 1977 when the body of his stepdaughter, Shirley Ann Ellington, was discovered underneath his car. Maxwell told a newspaper reporter that the car had fallen on her while she was changing a tire. Authorities were puzzled by the fact that the girl's hands were clean even though Maxwell claimed that she had removed the tire from the car. By this time, many locals were convinced that the reverend was a murderer.

Maxwell's seemingly charmed existence came to an abrupt end. Shirley Ann Ellington's funeral was held at a funeral home in Alexander City on the third Saturday of June. Halfway through the service, a woman stood up and screamed, "You killed my sister, and now you gonna pay for it!" Almost simultaneously, Shirley Ann Ellington's uncle, thirty-six-year-old truck driver Robert Louis Burns, fired his pistol three times in Maxwell's direction, killing him. At the time, Maxwell was sitting in front of Burns. Ironically, Burns hired Maxwell's lawyer, Tom Radney, to defend him. In his opening statement, Radney admitted that his client had killed Maxwell, but he insisted that Maxwell was innocent by reason of insanity. Many of the people sitting in the courtroom were certain that Burns was innocent, and by the end of the trial, Radney had convinced the jury that Burns was innocent by reason of insanity. Burns was committed to Bryce Hospital, a state mental hospital in Tuscaloosa, for assessment. Following Burns's release a few weeks later, he returned to work at his trucking firm. Tom Radney was so popular following his successful defense of Burns that he was named Alexander City's "Man of the Year" for 1978.

The story does not end here, however. In 1978, Harper Lee, the author of *To Kill a Mockingbird*, arrived in Alexander City to conduct research for a true-crime novel based on the alleged crimes of Reverend Maxwell. She immediately contacted Tom Radney, who gave her his case files. For the next several years, Lee communicated with Radney regarding the progress of the book project. Radney's widow, Madolyn Radney, still has the four opening pages of Lee's book, which she sent the attorney. On the top of the first page was the handwritten title, "The Reverend." The manuscript is

Harper Lee, shown receiving the Medal of Freedom from President George W. Bush in 2007, considered writing a true-crime book about accused murderer Reverend Willie Maxwell from Alexander City. *Eric Drapers.*

typed, with the exception of the "b's," which were handwritten, apparently because the "b" key was stuck. Although Lee insisted that she had written more, the Radney family received only those four pages. Burns, who had been interviewed twice by Lee, said that she decided against publishing the book because it would incriminate a number of people in Alexander City.

DANIEL WEBSTER SANDERSON'S LONELY DEATH

Some murders, especially those committed in small towns, are so heinous that they shake the community to its very core. The murders of children are generally regarded to be the most horrible of these crimes. One such murder occurred in the little community of Hope Hull, Alabama, shortly after the end of the Civil War.

A story that appeared in the January 4, 1866 edition of the *Daily Advertiser* reported the murder of a fourteen-year-old boy named Daniel Sanderson, who was the son of Almon Sanderson. Daniel and his family lived five miles east of Letohatchee, and on the evening of December 27, 1865, Daniel asked his father to accompany him to the roosting spot of a flock of turkeys. Almon was not feeling well and told his son that he would have to go hunting by himself. Dismayed, Daniel grabbed his gun and walked into the swamp.

After the sun went down, Almon became concerned that his son had not returned. He asked his neighbors to join him in searching for Daniel. They found him lying in a palmetto thicket about one and a half miles from his home. The men discovered evidence of a fierce struggle that led to the boy's head being struck so hard that, in the words of the reporter, "his brains oozed out of his head and on the ground near him....His gun was found loaded and bloody....The stock was found broken over his head." The body had been stomped on and lacerated after the poor child had fallen. He was found around 10:00 a.m. living, but unconscious. He had evidently been attacked the evening before and crawled about ten feet from where he fell. Who can tell the horror of that cold and dreary night? What must have been the feelings of his father when he raised him up in his arms and found that his darling boy had been lying, bleeding and dying all night within calling distance of the house?

Daniel lingered on until Friday at midnight. Almon Sanderson immediately suspected one of his servants, whom his son had caught stealing corn from the corncrib. Daniel had forced the boy to return the corn to his father, who chastised him severely. During an investigation of the servants' quarters, authorities found human blood on the shirt and apron of two other servants. The fate of the three servants accused of murdering Daniel Webster Sanderson is unknown.

The parents of little Daniel Webster were so outraged by the senseless death of their son that they hired a stonemason to engrave an account of his murder on his tombstone:

Daniel Webster Sanderson's tombstone in the Tabernacle Cemetery in Hope Hull, Alabama, recounts the grisly murder of a fourteen-year-old boy. *Alice T. Carter.*

Sacred
To the memory of
Daniel Webster
Son of
A. & E. Sanderson
Born May 19th, 1851,
Was brutally murdered
By three Negroes
Dec. 27th, 1865.
Aged 13 yr's. 8mo's
& 8 days.
He was followed and
Murdered 1½ miles from
his father's house.
When found, his head
Was beaten to pieces
With his own Rifle, and
His brains oozing out.

Daniel Webster Sanderson was buried in the cemetery of the Tabernacle Methodist Church. Almon Sanderson donated the land, and he and his neighbors built the church on the Federal Road in 1846. In 1978, the church was turned over to the Tabernacle Historical Association, which restored the building and the cemetery. Without a doubt, the tombstone of Daniel Webster Sanderson is the cemetery's most famous monument.

HAZEL FARRIS: THE BESSEMER MUMMY

Some people have acquired more notoriety after their deaths than they had when they were alive. In 1995, the frozen corpse of a twelve-year-old girl nicknamed the "Inca Ice Maiden" was discovered on the summit of Mount Ampato in the Peruvian Andes. The traumatic injuries to her head suggested that Mummy Juanita, as the ice maiden is officially known, was a victim of human sacrifice. In 1922, archaeologist Howard Carter discovered the tomb of King Tut, the Egyptian boy king, which was almost perfectly intact and contained golden objects and other funerary items, as well as the mummy of King Tut, which is now on public display at the Valley of the Kings. A far less famous example of an accidental mummification was on display for many years at the Hall of History in Bessemer, Alabama.

Born in Bessemer in 1880, Hazel Farris moved to Lexington, Kentucky, when she was very young. While growing up, Hazel was as well known for her violent temper as she was for her great beauty. Hazel married when she was very young, and predictably, her relationship with her husband was turbulent to say the least. Legend has it that one day, Hazel walked into the front room where her husband was reading the newspaper and announced that she needed a new hat. When he refused to buy it for her, she produced a pistol from the folds of her dress and shot him. Three policemen who were walking by heard the shots, and when they ran into the house to investigate,

The mummified remains of Hazel Farris were displayed in the Bessemer Hall of History from 1974 to 1981. *Alan Brown.*

91

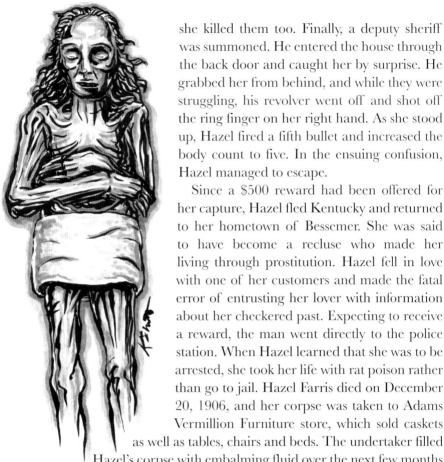

she killed them too. Finally, a deputy sheriff was summoned. He entered the house through the back door and caught her by surprise. He grabbed her from behind, and while they were struggling, his revolver went off and shot off the ring finger on her right hand. As she stood up, Hazel fired a fifth bullet and increased the body count to five. In the ensuing confusion, Hazel managed to escape.

Since a $500 reward had been offered for her capture, Hazel fled Kentucky and returned to her hometown of Bessemer. She was said to have become a recluse who made her living through prostitution. Hazel fell in love with one of her customers and made the fatal error of entrusting her lover with information about her checkered past. Expecting to receive a reward, the man went directly to the police station. When Hazel learned that she was to be arrested, she took her life with rat poison rather than go to jail. Hazel Farris died on December 20, 1906, and her corpse was taken to Adams Vermillion Furniture store, which sold caskets as well as tables, chairs and beds. The undertaker filled Hazel's corpse with embalming fluid over the next few months in an effort to preserve it until somebody showed up to claim it. For the next few months, it became readily apparent that her corpse was drying up and turning into a mummy. In fact, within a year, her corpse looked more like that of a one-hundred-year-old woman than that of a twenty-five-year-old redhead, and no one could understand why.

Mummies were a rarity back then, so the furniture store displayed her body. After a few months, a carny named O.C. Brooks purchased her for twenty-five dollars in 1907 and displayed her in traveling sideshows throughout the South for over forty years, charging people ten cents to see her. O.C. Brooks left the mummy to his grand-nephew, Luther, on the condition that he used all of the money he made through the exhibition for charitable purposes. Luther continued to display the mummy and used the proceeds to build churches throughout Tennessee. Then in 1974, the Bessemer Hall of History came to possess the mummy and charged people fifty cents a head to see her until 1981, when Hazel was retired due to deterioration. Tina Jones, the director of the Division of Economic Development and Outreach at the University of West Alabama, said that, as a child, she viewed the mummy of Hazel Farris on a school trip and had nightmares for several days afterward.

For many years, Hazel's rapid mummification was an unsolved mystery. One theory proposed by a historian was that at the turn of the century, many funeral home directors used arsenic to embalm bodies because it was more effective than formaldehyde. The effects of the arsenic injected into the corpse by the mortician, combined with the effects of the arsenic Hazel ingested in the rat poison, caused her body to dehydrate. Another theory was offered in 2002 in episode twelve of *The Mummy Road Show*, a National Geographic television series. In the episode, an autopsy revealed that Hazel Farris's corpse had been immersed in arsenic, refuting the legend that she had ingested it. Her dissected remains were cremated following the autopsy.

MYSTERIOUS DISAPPEARANCES

THE STRANGE CASE OF ORION WILLIAMSON

American history is filled with tales of unsolved disappearances. In 1930, Judge Joseph Crater, a justice of the New York Supreme Court, climbed into a taxi after attending a Broadway show and dining with friends. He was never seen again. The world lost all contact with aviatrix Amelia Earhart when she and her co-pilot, Wiley Post, were flying off the coast of New Guinea. American Labor Union leader Jimmy Hoffa vanished on July 30, 1975, amid rumors that he was the victim of a mob hit. However, no disappearance is more bizarre that of an Alabama farmer named Orion Williamson

By the mid-nineteenth century, Orion Williamson was on his way to achieving his version of the American dream. He and his wife and child were living on a farm outside of Selma with money he had worked hard to save. One July morning in 1854, he left his house, just as he had done many times before, and entered the realm of Alabama folklore

The story goes that he was sitting on his front porch with his wife and son when he noticed several of his horses standing in the field. He informed his wife that he was going to lead the horses back to the barn and had reached the middle of his field when he completely vanished from sight. A few seconds earlier, Williamson had just turned to wave in the ankle-deep grass to his two acquaintances, Amour Wen and his son, James, as they drove past in a buggy.

In 1893, Ambrose Bierce wrote about the disappearance of Orion Williamson in a short story titled "The Difficulty of Crossing a Field." *John Herbert Evelyn Partington.*

The two men leaped from the buggy and hurried to the field to see what had happened to their friend. When they reached the spot where Williamson had disappeared, they were shocked to find that most of the grass was gone. A few minutes later, Mrs. Williamson also ran to the place where she had last seen her husband and began shouting his name. Dozens of local people took up the search in the afternoon, combing the field and the nearby woods. Even bloodhounds were unable to pick up Williamson's scent. A flock of reporters descended on Selma to report on what had become one of the nation's greatest mysteries. One reporter, Ambrose Bierce, wrote about the incident in a short story titled "The Difficulty of Crossing a Field" (1893). Before writing the story, Bierce had consulted with a German scientist, Dr. Maximillian Hern, who had written a book entitled *The Disappearance and Theory Thereof.* Bierce scoffed at Hern's theory that spots of "universal ether" could dissolve solid objects. Twenty years later, Bierce himself vanished south of the border in Mexico, where he had gone to interview the bandit Pancho Villa.

Interestingly enough, the story of Orion Williamson may have a connection to the disappearance of a Tennessee farmer named David Lang on September 23, 1880. In fact, the only major difference between the two tales is that Lang was walking into the barn to hitch up his mule when he vanished in front of his wife and child and two men in a buggy. Over the years, scores of researchers have attempted to verify the Lang disappearance, but to no avail. No newspaper accounts of the incident have been discovered, and no mention of David Lang's name has been found in census records. The earliest known account of Lang's disappearance appeared in an article written by mystery novel writer Stuart Palmer for *Fate Magazine* in 1953. Some researchers believe that Palmer rewrote Bierce's story in "The Difficulty of Crossing a Field." Ironically, the David Lang version of the story is much better known than the Williamson version.

AUSTIN MIZE AND THE GHOST SHIP *CYCLOPS*

The Liberty Presbyterian Church was organized in Odenville, Alabama, between the years of 1885 and 1889. In 1912, the church purchased the lot on which its building now stands from M. Wat Brown of the Odenville Land Company for $125. The name of one member of the Mize family, Austin Mize, is inscribed on a memorial marker in the Liberty Presbyterian Cemetery:

Forman Austin Mize
Feb 13, 1900
Lost on USS Cyclops
March 1918
Gone but not Forgotten
Son

The fate of Austin Mize is intertwined with one of history's greatest maritime mysteries.

The USS *Cyclops* was a 542-foot-long, 19,000-ton navy coaling ship. Richard Winer, author of *Ghost Ships*, describes the massive cargo ship: "[Its] skeletal frameworks of gantries, booms and other coal-handling apparatus, along with its twin side-by-side stacks, gave her the appearance

Austin Mize, a resident of Odenville, Alabama, was one of 306 crew members of the USS *Cyclops* who were lost at sea in March 1918. *Naval History and Heritage Command.*

of some prehistoric creature that had awakened from eons of sleep." The captain was Lieutenant Commander George W. Worley, who had commanded the ship since it was first launched in 1910. Worley was an imposing figure dressed in his long underwear and carrying a cane, and he was rarely seen without his derby hat. He was feared and hated by his men for his unreasonably strict rules. Worley was known to fly into blind rages and take out his wrath on some unsuspecting officer. On one of his "punishment days," Worley ordered a group of sailors who had violated his rules to run barefoot along the searing-hot decks of the ship.

On February 3, 1918, the USS *Cyclops* arrived in Rio, where it took on a load of eleven thousand tons of manganese ore. As the water level reached the safety load mark painted on the hull of the ship, Worley refused to batten the hatches. By the time the ship headed up the coast to Brazil, it was clearly overloaded. On February 22, the USS *Cyclops* received orders to sail from the island of Barbados to Baltimore. On March 5, the British ocean liner *Vestris* exchanged radio communications with the USS *Cyclops*. The radio controller onboard the *Cyclops* reported "fair weather" and "no difficulties." This was the *Cyclops's* last radio message.

Austin Mize had left Odenville in the winter of 1918 to enlist on the USS *Cyclops*, and just three days after celebrating his eighteenth birthday, he and the rest of the crew set sail from Rio de Janeiro into what is now known as the Bermuda Triangle. Mize and the other 305 other crew members disappeared sometime in March while heading to Maryland. An intensive sea search covered thousands of miles, but no trace of the ship or its crew was ever found. Theories as to why the USS *Cyclops* vanished range from storms and capsizing to German wartime activity. The death toll aboard the USS *Cyclops* represents the single largest loss of life in the history of the U.S. Navy that is unrelated to combat.

THE DISAPPEARANCE OF HARRIS RUFUS LOGGINS

Harris Rufus Loggins was born in Blount County in 1862 to Confederate soldier John C. Loggins and his wife, Sarah Ann Self Loggins. He married Dovie Lou Stephenson, the daughter of Alexander J. and Dicey Stephenson from Winston County, in 1892. Harris and Dovie Lou lived near Cordova in Walker County until 1910, when they moved back to Compton. For the remainder of his life, Harris worked as a farmer and raised his seven children with Dovie Lou. On February 21, 1939, eighty-year-old Harris Rufus Loggins got out of bed, dressed and walked out the front door just as he had been doing for decades. When he failed to return later that evening, his relatives told the sheriff's office that it was "not like him" to leave the house without telling anyone where he was going. The sheriff suggested that he may have walked down the road to visit some relatives, but his wife and children dismissed this explanation as being unlikely. A search party consisting of hundreds of volunteers combed the hills of Compton but found no trace of Loggins.

For over two months, no evidence pertaining to Loggins's disappearance was found. Then on May 10, a farmer named A.C. Posey was walking past his barn when he discovered what appeared to be a human thigh bone. Judging from the teeth marks, Posey assumed that the bone had been dug up by his dogs. Posey turned the bone over to a group of doctors who determined that it belonged to the body of an adult male who had been deceased for at least ninety days. Authorities conducted a second search, and this time, it was around Posey's property since it was where Harris was last seen. Two days later, family members and law enforcement found two human arm bones, but at the time, it was impossible to tell whether or not they were the remains of Harris Rufus Loggins because DNA analysis did not exist. The remainder of the skeleton was never found, the coroner's office never issued a death certificate and a monument to Harris Rufus Loggins has never been erected.

Over the years, a number of theories for Loggins's disappearance have been presented. Some people believe that he became disoriented in the mountains and died from exposure. Still others say that he lost his life through an untimely accident that prevented him from walking home. A few residents of Blount County insist that Harris Rufus Loggins was murdered and his body was thrown in a gorge. His widow, Dovie Lou Loggins, spent the remainder of her life on the Blount County and Jefferson line. She passed away on March 2, 1948, and is buried in Marvin's Chapel in Mount Pinson.

THE BRASHER–DYE MYSTERY

On March 3, 1956, two brothers, nineteen-year-old Billy Howard Dye and twenty-three-year-old Robert Earl Dye, and their thirty-eight-year-old cousin, Dan Brasher, were visiting a relative's house in the backwoods of Jefferson County. Later that evening, the young men drove down Crooked Creek Road to Robinwood outside of Morris, Alabama, in search of a party. They were never seen again.

Their families were not immediately alarmed when the boys failed to return the next day because they were in the habit of staying out late partying. Friends and relatives assumed that they were drying out in a local drunk tank somewhere and would eventually turn up with dirty clothes and splitting headaches. After several days, their cousin, Curtis Brasher, and his father began combing through all of the jails between Morris and Decatur, but no one knew what had happened to them. When the Brashers returned home empty-handed, they decided to file a missing person's report with the Jefferson County Sheriff's Department. Their families became even more concerned when the men, who had been part of a road crew building Highway 31 north of Birmingham, failed to pick up their paychecks. Over the next few weeks, search parties investigated a twenty- to twenty-five-square-mile area in Morris County. Suspecting that the men might have been the victims of foul play, the search parties began to scan abandoned mines, creeks, woods, wells, roads and caves. They even brought in an airplane to assist with the search, but no trace of the young men or Billy's 1947 dark green four-door Ford was ever found.

The sheriff and his deputies interviewed people living in the area where the men had vanished, but they gathered very little information from the "tight-lipped" community. Several people reported hearing gunshots the night the men disappeared. A neighbor who lived next to the Robinwood house, where the three men attended a party, claimed to have seen several men carrying buckets of water into the house. Some people speculated that the three men had been murdered while attempting to steal whiskey from local moonshiners. The investigators also "picked up" several rumors that a bulldozer was seen burying a 1947 dark green Ford around U.S. Highway 79, which was under construction at the time.

After the sheriff's department called off the investigation, Curtis Brasher embarked on his own one-man search for his relatives. Determined to keep interest in the case alive, Brasher wrote letters to state officials right up until he died in the 1980s. Because of Brasher's tireless efforts to locate the bodies of his loved ones, Sheriff Holt McDowell assigned Deputy Tom Ellison to the case. In November 1972, the State Highway Department began drilling near the construction site off Highway 79 where witnesses claimed to have seen a bulldozer burying a car seventeen years earlier. The drill produced a few metallic fragments, which could have been from a car. Encouraged by the find, Jefferson County employees spent the next three weeks digging at the site with shovels and removing the dirt with wheelbarrows. The only pieces of evidence discovered in the forty-foot-deep hole were patches of oil that may have come from an automobile. On December 1, digging was halted. Three years later, Commissioner Tom Gloor ordered county works to comb the other side of the highway using U.S. Navy metal detectors. However, nothing other than a few pieces of metal were found.

Over the next few years, attention on the case shifted to the involvement of local moonshiners in the disappearance of the young men. A state investigator named O.M. Rains stated in a 1984 *Post Herald* article that the Dye brothers had been killed at the Robinwood party and that their cousin was murdered a few days later and interred in a cemetery somewhere in the Morris area. In a 1990s article, Deputy Tom Ellison accused Sheriff McDowell of removing him from the case in the 1970s because he was close to solving it. Like Ellison, Rains was convinced that the sheriff had hampered the investigation because of his connections to local bootleggers. Ellison's and Rains's allegations were never substantiated.

The Case of the Missing Sunday School Teacher

Ruth Murphree Dorsey was, to all appearances, an ordinary southern woman. She graduated from Randolph-Macon Women's College with a degree in education. Dorsey taught mathematics and French until her marriage in 1928. She also played the organ and taught Sunday school at Hopewell Methodist Church. Following the death of her husband in 1965, Dorsey worked for the First National Bank. Her retirement was cut short in a way that still baffles authorities.

On August 17, 1974, the town of Opelika was rocked by the disappearance of Ruth Murphree Dorsey. Witnesses recalled that on that day, the five-foot-four-inch-tall woman was wearing a flowery blouse, a long, brown skirt and she may have been wearing sunglasses. According to the police report, she pulled into the gas station at the Spring Villa Grocery between 4:30 and 5:00 p.m. in her 1972 Ford Galaxy. She told the gas attendant that she was "putting up peas" when she received a phone call from a relative. Dorsey said that she needed to gas up her car so that she could pick up one of her "kin." At 6:00 p.m., she was seen turning into her driveway. This was the last known sighting of Ruth Murphree Dorsey.

Dorsey was not reported missing until the next day when she did not show up for Sunday school or church services. Authorities were immediately dispatched to her home and were surprised to find the side door unlocked and the front door wide open. Walking inside, they discovered that her bed appeared not to have been slept in and her Bible and other materials had been carefully placed on the dining room table. Dorsey's three dogs, which, under normal conditions, would have rushed at intruders, were lying on the bathroom floor, shaking. Speaking to police about one of the canines, Dorsey's nephew, David Dorsey, said, "That was a dog that would eat you alive if you tried to come in while she was there." David also said that it was uncharacteristic of her to leave the doors unlocked. The police then located Dorsey's car, which was parked downtown in front of a house that she and her late husband had occupied. The door to this house was open as well. Dorsey did not appear to have entered the house recently. The car was discovered by Martha Smith and her cousins. Inside the car were Dorsey's eyeglasses and purse, which contained eleven dollars in cash. The keys were still in the ignition. Later, investigators reported that it appeared as if someone had left the car with the intention of coming back immediately after completing a short errand. David Dorsey's skin crawled as he watched the police search the car. "I'll never forget seeing that license plate. I thought, 'Oh, my God! She's in the trunk of that car.'" Police did not find Dorsey's body in the car, her home or anywhere on the Dorseys' 350-acre farm. Other statewide and out-of-state law enforcement agencies were contacted, including the FBI, but the investigation was impeded by a lack of forensic evidence. The family also consulted nationally known psychics Don and Dorothy Hudson, but the case remains unsolved.

At first, the police believed that Ruth Murphree Dorsey had simply left town for "greener pastures," but Dorsey's friends and family dismissed any suggestion that she had simply "run off." They told police that, as a rule, she told somebody she knew when she was leaving town. Legend has it that she was buried under the Farmers National Bank while it was being constructed. So far, neither that theory nor any of the others regarding Dorsey's disappearance has been confirmed.

IX
LEGENDARY PLACES

BEAR CREEK SWAMP

Located in Autauga County, Bear Creek Swamp is one of the most mysterious places in the entire state of Alabama. Some of the tales focus on a Creek village in the swamp. The Creeks were drawn to the swamp because they believed that the artesian well discovered in the swamp contained healing powers. The village was abandoned following the Creeks' forced evacuation in 1814. For years, the Creeks told stories of the "Little People," humanoid creatures, approximately four feet tall, who lived in the remote reaches of the swamp. Many of the whites who settled there in the first half of the nineteenth century were veterans of the Creek Indian War. Generations of teenagers have visited the swamp as a rite of passage, and they believe that the orbs flitting through the trees and bushes are the spirits of the swamp's early inhabitants.

The twentieth century has also contributed to the lore of the region. Young people bold enough to drive on County Road 3 through the swamp say that it is haunted by the spirit of a woman who lost her baby in the swamp. If you loudly exclaim, "We have your baby!" it is said that her ghost will respond in violent ways. One young man claimed to have heard something head in his direction through the brush before he was cut on the leg by the woman's ghost while trying to unlock his car door. Another "modern" entity that has been known to disrupt the tranquility of the swamp is a phantom car. A television station WSFA reporter described one of these unnerving encounters:

*Suddenly, we saw two cars' headlights coming from opposite directions. As
we backed off as far as we could to the side of the road, one of the cars
raced passed us....We were afraid that there would soon be a collision.
As we looked towards the other car, it slowly went past us in the opposite
direction. To our amazement, there was no collision or even a beeped horn.
There was no place for the speeding car to go except into the swamps. We
rewound the tape to see where the other car went and found no sign of the
speeding car, only the slow car from the other direction.*

One of the strangest stories connected to Bear Creek Swamp focuses on a bizarre discovery made in the swamp by the Autauga County Sheriff's Office in November 2014. While driving down County Road 3 to investigate a stolen vehicle report, Chief Deputy Joe Sedinger noticed several porcelain heads of dolls mounted atop bamboo stakes. Sedinger did not pay much attention to the dolls until news of the dolls made its way to social media. The sheriff's office notified the timber company that owned that part of the swamp about the dolls. When the timber company failed to respond, the sheriff decided it would be best to just go ahead and retrieve the dolls. Sedinger and several other deputies paddled around in a canoe and picked up the dolls. "I admit it looked kind of creepy," Sedinger said, laughing. "You could see them from the road." One of the locals in the courthouse who discussed the discovery of the dolls, Jan Taylor, said, "If somebody says they've seen a clown out there pulling up dolls, I'm never going to Autauga again."

THE FACE IN THE WINDOW OF THE PICKENS COUNTY COURTHOUSE

On April 5, 1865, Union general John T. Croxton ordered his troops to burn down the Pickens County Courthouse in Carrollton, Alabama. Following the Civil War, the citizens of Carrollton pooled together their resources and erected an impressive wooden courthouse. Then on November 16, 1976, the unthinkable occurred. The courthouse burned down a second time. Because the courthouse had come to represent the restoration of their dignity as a southern community, the residents of Carrollton demanded that justice be served. The sheriff, who was under a great deal of pressure to apprehend the culprit, concluded that the most likely suspect was a mean-spirited black man with a criminal history named Henry Wells. Wells was finally apprehended two years later by two brothers, H.C. and W.B. Sawls, on Bill McConner's plantation where he had been employed. By this time, a third structure had been erected. Determined that his prisoner would not fall victim to mob violence, the sheriff sequestered Wells in the garret of the new courthouse.

According to a version of the legend that appears in Kathryn Tucker Windham's book *13 Alabama Ghosts and Jeffrey*, Wells was sitting in the garret, peering from the north window, when he noticed a mob congregating around the courthouse. Fearing that he was about to be lynched, Wells summoned up the courage to confront his accusers. As lightning flashed across the sky, Wells proclaimed, "I am an innocent man. If you hang me, I will be with you always." The members of the mob, who were unable to hear Wells, rushed up the stairs of the courthouse and dragged him downstairs to a large pecan tree where they lynched him.

The next day, two members of the lynch mob were walking down the sidewalk past the courthouse when they spied a spectral face staring down at them from one of the panes of the north garret window. The men dashed up the stairs and were surprised to find the room empty. Over the years, the face in the window has resisted every attempt by nature and man to obliterate it. In 1929, a hailstorm destroyed every window in

The bizarre image in the garret window of the Pickens County Courthouse is reputed to be the face of Henry Wells, who was incarcerated for the crime of arson. *Marilyn Brown.*

the building except the one imprinted with Henry Wells's image. People have tried to remove the face by scrubbing the window with soap and water and gasoline, but to no avail.

The historical record of the burning of the Pickens County Courthouse is much more mundane. According to an article appearing in the *West Alabamian* on January 30, 1878, Henry Wells was shot twice by the Sawls brothers on Bill McConner's plantation on January 29, 1878. Wells had been implicated by Bill Burkhalter, who had committed a number of crimes with him. Burkhalter told the authorities that he saw Wells enter the probate office, light several candles and leave. Afterward, Wells told Burkhalter that he had "set the damned thing on fire." Burkhalter and Wells were both confined in the county jail. Henry Wells died of his gunshot wounds a few days later. The windows in the courthouse were not installed until February.

Despite the weight of the historical facts in the case, Alabamians have never let the truth get in the way of a good story. Today, visitors to Carrollton can get a clear view of the infamous face in the courthouse window by looking through a telescope that is mounted across the street from the courthouse. Hundreds of people visit Carrollton each year to view and photograph the eerie image.

BIRMINGHAM'S RAM-HEADED STORYTELLER FOUNTAIN

The term "urban legend" refers to apocryphal tales that are presented as being true, which supposedly took place in a modern setting. As a rule, the stories contain supernatural, humorous or bizarre elements. "Urban legend" was a term coined by English professor and author Jan Harold Brunvand in his book *The Vanishing Hitchhiker: American Urban Legends & Their Meanings* (1981). In this book and others that followed, Brunvand attempted to show that legends are not generated only by people who live in rural or primitive societies. A good example of an urban legend is the supposedly true story behind the Five Points South Storyteller Fountain in Birmingham, Alabama.

Located in front of the Highlands United Methodist Church where Twentieth Street South, Eleventh Court South and Magnolia Avenue converge, the Five Points South Fountain was created by local artist Frank Fleming. The whimsical bronze fountain depicts a ram-headed storyteller who is seated upon a log reading from an undisclosed book to a group of frogs and other wild creatures seated on circular platforms. The man-like figure holds a staff topped with an owl. The animals are enveloped in swirling streams of water.

The fountain was commissioned in 1983 through the Birmingham Arts Association by Jane McRae as a memorial for her son, Malcom McRae. A Birmingham art dealer and anthropologist, McRae had been murdered by Gerald Wayne Lawley, who attempted to conceal his body in the woods of Helena, Alabama. With the encouragement of Cecil Roberts and Mayor Richard Arrington, Mrs. McRae's original idea of a garden with a tiled border morphed into a sculptural fountain. Special public events were held to raise money for the statue, including a dinner hosted by Chef Frank Stitt at Highland's Bar and Grill. Fleming had originally envisioned using a lion as a central figure to represent Malcom McRae, but as work progressed, he decided to change it to a ram. Fleming called his work *The Storyteller*. The fountain itself was installed and activated in 1992 after the capital was raised to complete the project.

Fleming's vision of the storytelling fountain as a "peaceable kingdom" was shattered almost from the outset. When the fountain was unveiled on October 8, 1991, a heckler shouted that the statue was "the work of the devil." Even before the dedication, some people said that the goat-headed man was a satanic figure. Others claimed that the five frogs listening to the

Frank Fleming's sculpture *The Storyteller*, located at 2000 Eleventh Avenue South in the Five Points section of Birmingham, has spawned rumors of satanic connections. *Alan Brown.*

storyteller were arranged at the points of a satanic pentagram. Initially, Fleming was not bothered by the negative publicity because there was so much innocence in the sculpture. However, once the satanic story began to spread, Fleming became depressed. When television crews began showing up at his house and asking him about his religious beliefs, he became so alarmed that he removed skulls and anything else that could have been perceived as satanic from his walls.

The public perception of Fleming's creation as being satanic still exists. On May 5, 2018, I traveled to the Five Points section of Birmingham to photograph the fountain. On this particular day, several young men were displaying religious art just a few feet from the fountain. After I had taken several pictures, I began to walk away when one of the men said, "Check your photographs. I bet they will all be blank." I told him that I would look at them when I returned to my car. All of the photographs turned out all right.

THE AVE MARIA GROTTO

Many of Alabama's tourist attractions are very well known. Thousands of people have driven down to Mobile to tour the USS *Alabama*. History-minded travelers visit Fort Morgan in Gulf Shores, the Civil Rights Institute in Birmingham and the Civil Rights Memorial in Montgomery. Music lovers flock to the W.C. Handy Home Museum in Florence. However, the strangest tourist destination by far is the Ave Maria Grotto in Cullman.

This strange collection of miniature buildings was the brainchild of a Benedictine monk named Brother Joseph Zoettl. Born in Bavaria in 1878, Brother Joseph immigrated to northern Alabama as a teenager. The diminutive immigrant stood under five feet tall, weighed under one hundred pounds and was afflicted with a slight hunchback as the result of a childhood accident. In 1897, he took his vows at the newly built Benedictine monastery of St. Bernard. Four years later, he was put in charge of the abbey's powerhouse because of a rule that forbade anyone with a physical disability from being ordained as a priest. Watching gauges turned out to be dreadfully boring, especially for someone with a very creative disposition. To pass the time, he began making small replicas of buildings and religious statues. By his own estimate, he created over five thousand of these pieces, which were sold in the gift shop.

The most striking of his creations was a replica of Holy Land structures, which he called "Little Jerusalem." By the early 1930s, however, he had become weary of his hobby. "I told Abbot Bernard I was getting old and could hardly do much anymore," Brother Joseph pleaded. "But he would not listen, so I started work and had plenty to do." In 1932, Brother Joseph started a very ambitious project in a four-acre abandoned quarry on the abbey's grounds. Until his death in 1961, Brother Joseph filled the old quarry with 125 miniature reproductions of some of the most famous buildings in the world. Mostly using cast-off materials, such as bicycle reflectors, beads, spools, pipes, plastic animals, costume jewelry, seashells, rocks, marbles, mirrors, watch crystals, pill bottles and copper commode floats, Brother Joseph fashioned a world in miniature. Constructed into a steep hillside are clusters of buildings, such as St. Peter's Basilica, the Sanctuary of Our Lady of Lourdes, the Monte Cassino Abbey, the empty tomb of Jesus Christ and an assortment of religious scenes. Secular scenes include the Roman Colosseum, the catacombs, the Leaning Tower of Pisa, German castles, Spanish missions, South African shrines and Hansel and Gretel's Temple of the Fairies.

Left: This is a statue of Brother Joseph Zoettl, who began his monastic work as director of the powerhouse. He started making his cement miniature buildings in 1918 to pass the time. Brother Joseph began work on the Ave Maria Grotto in 1932. *Alan Brown.*

Below: St. Peter's is the largest miniature in the Roman Group, which the accompanying sign describes as the most "awe-inspiring" section of the Ave Maria Grotto. Above St. Peter's is the Abbey of Monte Cassino, the first Benedictine monastery. *Alan Brown.*

The section known as Little Jerusalem is one of Brother Joseph's earliest works. Originally located in the monastery recreation grounds, the miniatures were moved to their present location in 1934. *Alan Brown.*

Known as one of the Seven Wonders of the Ancient World, the Hanging Gardens of Babylon were constructed by King Nebuchadnezzar in Babylon in 3,000 BC. *Alan Brown.*

Brother Joseph was eighty years old when he made the Lourdes Shrine, commemorating the appearance of the Virgin Mary to fourteen-year-old Bernadette Soubirious in a small cave on February 11, 1858. *Alan Brown.*

The most amazing aspect of this world in miniature is the way in which it was made. He had visited only two of the sites he had miniaturized: St. Martin's Church in Landshut, Bavaria, and a castle not far from the church. Because he was a shy man who hated to travel outside of Alabama, he copied most of his buildings from photographs on postcards and descriptions in books. Experts on architecture marvel at the accurate proportions of his models and his attention to even the smallest details.

Brother Joseph labored on his miniature world with nothing more than basic hand tools while continuing to run the power plant for seventeen hours a day, seven days a week. Frail health and the encroachment of old age did little to slow him down. By the time Brother Joseph died at the age of eighty, he had created not only Cullman's biggest tourist attraction but also a source of inspiration and awe.

ENTERPRISE'S MONUMENT TO THE BOLL WEEVIL

The boll weevil is a beetle measuring approximately six millimeters in length that destroys the boll containing the cotton on a cotton plant. The boll weevil was first introduced to the United States from Mexico in 1892. The boll weevil made its way to Mobile in 1910. By 1916, the pest had infested cotton farms throughout the entire state. At this time, Alabama's economy was based primarily on cotton production. Most cotton farmers lost between 60 and 70 percent of their crops. Consequently, Alabama's economy suffered mightily. Annual losses fluctuated between $20 and $40 million. Farmers tried to eradicate the beetle by conducting controlled burns and using homemade insecticides. In 1918, an insecticide named calcium arsenate was introduced to cotton fields in Alabama with some success, and it was used through mid-1942. However, the only method that really worked was switching over to other crops, such as peanuts. Oddly enough, this destructive insect is memorialized in a monument in Enterprise.

According to the official version of the tale, the Mexican boll weevil began infesting the local cotton crop in 1915. One year later, cotton production was reduced by one-third. In desperation, farmers were forced to diversify. They began planting crops that did not deplete the soil of nutrients as cotton had done, such as corn, hay, sugarcane, potatoes and peanuts. Before long, farmers were greatly increasing the productivity of their land. In fact, in 1917, over one million bushels of peanuts were harvested. To commemorate the unexpected benefits of the devastating infestation, an Enterprise businessman and city council member named Roscoe O. (Bon) Fleming proposed erecting a statue to the boll weevil. He commissioned the white marble figure from an Italian sculptor. Originally, the neoclassical statue held a fountain over its head; the beetle was added thirty years later. The total cost of the monument was $1,795, and Fleming paid approximately half the cost. The plaque in front of the statue reads, "In profound appreciation of the boll weevil and what it has done as the herald of prosperity, this monument was erected by the citizens of Enterprise, Coffee County, Alabama."

The unofficial backstory behind the construction of the monument is even more amusing. In 1919, downtown Enterprise had two renovation projects going on at the same time. Traffic lights were being installed, and a twelve-sided fountain was being constructed in the middle of Main Street. Every day, street workers were bombarded with questions from passersby. On one particularly hot summer's day, a man walked over to a workman and asked, "What are you all doin'?" Peeved at having to answer the same question day

Legend has it that the boll weevil monument was erected by the citizens of Enterprise, Alabama, in 1919 to commemorate the state's boll weevil infestation of 1915. *Martin Lewison.*

after day, the worker replied, "We're puttin' up a statue to the boll weevil." He was overheard by another man walking down the sidewalk. Convinced that what he had just heard was true, the man contacted a reporter from the *Montgomery Advertiser* and told him that Enterprise was building a statue to the boll weevil. When the town fathers read about the statue in the next issue of the *Montgomery Advertiser*, the mayor said, "Well, boys, if it's in the newspaper, I guess we have to do it." Many people living in Alabama accept the fanciful story as the gospel truth, probably because legends can be much more fun to relay than the facts.

THE CRYING PECAN TREE OF NEEDHAM, ALABAMA

All over the world, people have viewed trees as homes for spirits. Sacred groves appear throughout the Old Testament. The ancient Romans read omens into trees. The Celts were so obsessed with trees that they developed an alphabet based on them. In Eastern countries, people hung gifts on trees. Shrines were built under trees in India to honor the spirits. Cloth or pieces of paper were hung from trees growing next to sacred wells in England. In a number of cultures, cutting down a tree that houses ghosts is believed to bring bad luck. The possibility that ghosts may have taken up residence in a pecan tree in a small town in Alabama in the 1980s became the basis for intensive media attention.

On April 12, 1981, a resident of Needham, Alabama, named Linnie Jenkins was standing several yards away from the seventy-five-foot-tall pecan tree in her front yard when she heard what sounded like the soft cries of a dreaming dog. She walked over to the tree and was surprised that the sound was coming from the inside. She returned to the house and told her family to come outside. Thinking that a puppy or some other small creature was trapped inside the tree, her sons sawed through the hollow roots but found nothing. "We even hit the sides of the tree to see if our noise made a difference," Ms. Jenkins said. "But it didn't." After digging several holes in the yard in a futile effort to find the source of the noises, she contacted Fred Childers, the editor of the *Choctaw Advocate*, and asked him to come to her place. Childers picked up his portable cassette tape recorder and drove out to Linnie Jenkins's front yard. He walked around the tree and recorded the sounds for a few minutes before returning to his office. Childers wrote up the story of the Jenkinses' strange tree and published it in the next edition of the newspaper. CNN, which had recently started up in Atlanta, sent a camera crew to the sleepy little West Alabama town to cover the story. As a result of the mounting publicity, hundreds of tourists flocked to Needham.

After a few days, Mrs. Jenkins decided to capitalize on her tree's notoriety by charging visitors fifty cents a head to listen to the tree. So many cars lined the narrow road that the local sheriff had to be called twice to clear the congestion. According to Mrs. Jenkins, the crowds peaked around Easter when the family had four hundred people in the yard at one time. Sheriff's deputy Kenneth Crenshaw estimated that over the next few weeks, thousands of people made their way to Lizzie Jenkins's property. Approximately one month after Mrs. Jenkins first contacted Childers, the noises began to fade away. A hole was dug at the base of the tree, and a copper tube was inserted in the wood to make it easy to hear the eerie cries. By April 30, the sounds had vanished completely.

In the aftermath of all the hoopla surrounding the crying pecan tree, a number of explanations were offered by locals and area experts. Mrs. Jenkins's neighbors told her that her house was built on top of a Native American burial ground. The whimpering sounds, they said, were produced by the restless spirits of the Native Americans who lay under the house. A forester for the American Can Co. named Allen Bruce believed that the souring of rotting wood produced gasses that seeped through slits in the tree. One whimsical commentator posited that the noises were the cries of seals swimming in an underground ocean. To this day, there is no generally accepted explanation for the strange sounds.

WHAT IS UNDERNEATH BIRMINGHAM'S BOTANICAL GARDENS?

As American cities grew, more and more early cemeteries became lost in the midst of urban sprawl. In 1997, excavations at Duane Street and Elk Street in Manhattan uncovered an African burial ground. Since the 1690s, as many as twenty thousand slaves were interred here, most in unmarked grades. In August 2006, the construction of a fiberoptic line at the Haunter Army Airfield in Savannah, Georgia, discovered a previously unknown cemetery consisting of thirty-seven graves. Birmingham's lost cemetery lies in the middle of one of the city's most popular tourist areas.

In 1822 and 1855, respectively, William Pullen and Joseph Byars were granted three parcels on the south slope of Red Mountain. On February 16, 1889, the City of Birmingham purchased the first eighty acres from the Irondale Company for use as a cemetery for indigent people. Some

Birmingham's Botanical Gardens are located on top of the old Red Mountain Cemetery, in which 4,711 convicts, indigent people and victims of disease are interred. *Alan Brown.*

burials, however, took place before the city acquired the property. On August 31, 1896, Birmingham bought additional acres from William Hickman and Alfred Eubank. Red Mountain Cemetery, as it was called, was located west of Cahaba Road. Between 1888 and 1909, over 4,711 people were buried here. Most of them were convicts, victims of disease in area pest houses and people whose families had not arranged for a burial. A smallpox hospital was also housed here at one time. Except for a single grave stone with the name "Annie" crudely chiseled into it, the graves were unmarked. Annie, it turns out, died of septicemia in 1890 at age fifty-eight. Only a few large rocks marked the boundaries of the cemetery.

In 1934, Mayor George B. Ward dedicated the abandoned cemetery as a city park named Lane Park in honor of Mayor Lane. Through the efforts of the Birmingham Federation of Garden Clubs and the Works Progress Administration, the Lane Park Arboretum was established on the property. The most significant improvements were the establishment of the Birmingham Zoo in 1955 and the opening of the Birmingham Botanical Gardens in 1962.

It is said that human remains were uncovered when workers were digging the pond at the Botanical Gardens. *Alan Brown.*

The existence of the old potter's field was largely unknown until the 1960s, when a number of bones were exhumed in the rose garden and the pond. The bones of one skeleton were particularly well preserved. Workers uncovered a number of artifacts as well, including shoelace tips, flint chips and a broken bottle with the raised letters "Birmingham." Gary Gerlach, an archivist for the Birmingham Public Library, said that it is difficult to determine the location of the graves because a map of the cemetery has never been found. He said that no caskets dating back to the 1890s were found during the construction of the zoo because they would be nothing more than a layer of dirt today. Today, representatives from the Birmingham Zoo and the Botanical Gardens work only with contractors who follow the proper procedures and policies in the event that human remains are uncovered. A spokesperson for the Botanical Gardens said that tour guides mention the Red Mountain Cemetery because it is an important part of the city's history.

MOUNT NEBO CEMETERY

From all appearances, Mount Nebo Baptist Church in Clarke County is just like any other small country church in Alabama. What sets it apart, though, is its cemetery. Three of the headstones are adorned by "death masks" made by Isaac Nettles Sr. (1885–1957). Nettles fashioned four death masks from mud molds that were formed on the faces of his subjects before they died. The casts were then transferred to plaster of Paris, and after it had hardened, he attached the death masks to the tombstone.

Three of Nettles's tombstones still survive. One of these tombstones marks the grave of his relative, Angel Ezella Nettles. The image of her face is still fairly well preserved. Manuel Burell's tombstone has the death mask of his face as well as the hand-drawn outline of a shirt with buttons. Burell's name and "Died 1946" are inscribed on the tombstone. The top part of the concrete tombstone has been damaged by vandals. Interestingly enough, Nettles's daughters are not buried at Mount Nebo, but the tombstone of Nettles's wife, Korean, who died in 1933, is the most elaborate of his existing creations. The narrow tombstone features the death masks of their three daughters—Pauline, Marie and Clara. The bottom death mask has been heavily damaged by the effects of rain. The fourth tombstone was the largest. It featured a life-sized, upper-torso image of his mother, Selena, who died in 1940. The tombstone was destroyed by Hurricane Frederick in 1979, and nothing remains except for the base of the tombstone.

All of the tombstones have weathered over time. Kerry Reed, the director of the Clarke County Historical Society, learned that repairing the death masks would reduce their value as folk art, so she decided to allow them to deteriorate naturally. Photographs have been taken to preserve the images of the faces for posterity. The church installed a gate to reduce traffic at night and, hopefully, vandalism as well.

HAL'S KINGDOM

Hal's Lake is located just north of the convergence of the Tombigbee and Alabama Rivers in Clarke County, and in 1939, a field worker for the Works Progress Administration named Mary A. Poole passed on a folk tale that reveals the origin of the lake's name. The story goes that a slave named Hal, who had run away from a Mississippi plantation in the late 1840s, settled in the isolated area around the lake. This turned out to be an ideal hiding place because of the thick canebrake and the abundance of wild game. Hal supplemented his diet with food he procured from nearby plantations. Before long, Hal encouraged other escaped slaves to join him. Only a few of their owners bothered tracking them down because of the large number of slaves who had made their way to freedom in the North through the Underground Railroad. The little colony around the lake soon came to be known in the slave community as "Hal's Kingdom." Hal demanded nothing but blind loyalty from his "subjects."

The settlement thrived for several years until one of the runaway slaves refused to submit to Hal's authority. Hal punished the unruly subject and returned him to his planation. Eager for revenge, the slave disclosed the location of Hal's Kingdom to his master, who then convinced his neighbors to form a raiding party and descend on Hal's Kingdom. The vigilantes broke up the community and left behind nothing but oral tales of the lakeside sanctuary. Hal's fate is unknown, but in one version of the tale, Hal was killed in the raid on his "kingdom." According to another variant, Hal was returned to his plantation in Mississippi.

The version of the tale that is posted on the Clarke County Historical Museum's website adds a few details to the WPA version. In this version, Hal was a slave who lived on Colonel Alex Holinger's planation in Port Bayou before escaping and settling in Hal's Kingdom. Within five years, his little commune included twenty runaway slaves. Hal's Kingdom entered a dangerous period in its short history when the slaves began stealing from nearby river plantations to prove to their owners that they had not escaped to the North on the Underground Railroad. One of the planters captured a runaway named Joe who agreed to lead him and his friends to Hal's Kingdom. After taking the men to the wrong bayou, which is now called "Joe's Bayou," he was forced to take them to Hal's Lake. The slaves fired on their former owners from a fortress made of cypress logs. During the short battle, Hal and three other slaves were killed, and the remaining slaves were returned to their respective plantations.

OAK MOUNTAIN TUNNEL

John Henry is immortalized in an American work song that celebrates the almost superhuman aspects of the "steel driving man." John Henry achieved widespread fame for his ability to hammer drills into rock and make holes for dynamite. Legend has it that John Henry finally met his match in a race against a steam-powered rock drilling machine during the construction of the tunnel for the C&O Railway Tunnel. John Henry won, but the stress was too much for his mighty heart, and he died with a hammer in his hand.

A number of different locations have been suggested as the site of the contest, including the Lewis Tunnel in Virgina and the Big Bend Tunnel in West Virginia. However, according to John Garst, a professor from the University of Georgia–Athens, Alabama was the actual setting of the steel driving race. In this variant of the tale, John Henry was actually an ex-slave from Copiah County, Mississippi, named John Henry Dabney. Between 1887 and 1888, Dabney worked on a railroad gang that dug tunnels through the Oak and Coosa Mountains as part of the C&W Railway extension. The man in charge of the project, Captain Dabney, was the son of John Henry Dabney's former owner. Captain Dabney bet a steam-drill salesman that John Henry Dabney could beat the steam drill in a race. On September 20, 1887, John Henry Dabney beat the steam drill, but he collapsed and died afterward from a ventricular rupture as his wife cradled his head in her arms. Several of the informants who contributed to this variant were railroad men who worked on the Coosa and Oak Mountain Tunnels. Further evidence in support of the Oak Mountain location was provided by a road superintendent for the Seaboard Air Line Railroad during the first half of the twentieth century named E.L. Voyles, who wrote in his journal that trains passing through Oak Mountain Tunnel blew their whistles in honor of John Henry. Voyles added that many railroad men were overcome with uneasy feelings inside the tunnel and that "most central engineers believed that John's ghost haunted Oak Tunnel."

Oak Mountain Tunnel is located near Leeds approximately fifteen miles east of Birmingham. Legend has it that a steel rod lying on the floor of one of the entrances is undeniable proof that the race actually took place at Oak Mountain Tunnel. Perhaps someday, a foolhardy explorer will be willing to risk his or her life to rewrite history by retrieving the—possibly apocryphal—steel rod.

Blakeley's Legendary Oaks

In 1814, Josiah Blakeley founded the riverfront town of Blakeley. Within a few years, Blakeley had become a thriving port city with docks, warehouses, a hotel, a courthouse and private residences owned by its four thousand residents. Blakeley served as the county seat of Baldwin County until its population was decimated by the yellow fever epidemics of 1822, 1826 and 1828. By the time the Battle of Blakeley—the last major battle of the Civil War—was fought there on April 9, 1865, Blakeley had fallen into decay. The county seat was moved to Daphne in 1868.

The ghost town of Blakeley is now part of Historic Blakeley State Park. Nothing much remains of the town aside from a grove of majestic live oaks that once lined the streets. According to legend, court was once held under one of these trees, which has since fallen down. Judge Toumlin is said to have presided over the court while sitting on one of the tree's limbs, and the jurors sat in and around its branches. The first hanging in Blakeley was carried out at a tree located near the site of Washington Square. Not surprisingly, this tree is now known as "The Hanging Tree."

X

UNIVERSITY LEGENDS

THE LADY WHO SAVED THE PRESIDENT'S MANSION AT THE UNIVERSITY OF ALABAMA

In 1838, the trustees of the University of Alabama set aside funds for the construction of the President's Mansion on a plot of land connected to the south side of the Quad. Architect Michael Barry designed the house in the Greek Revival style. Basil Manly Sr., the first resident of the mansion, was the university's second president. The Alabama legislature criticized President Manly and the Board of Trustees for the house's lavish style. Landon Garland, the third president, witnessed the burning of the university and near destruction of the President's Mansion. He argued for the conversion of the university to the military system in order to combat what he perceived to be the school's discipline problems. By doing so, Garland turned the university into a military target when Union general John Croxton's cavalrymen attacked Tuscaloosa on April 3, 1865. A home guard composed primarily of teenaged boys and old men attempted to halt the Yankees' advance by tearing up the planks on the bridge leading into Tuscaloosa from Northport. Colonel James Murfee marched the three hundred remaining cadets, most of whom were fifteen and sixteen years old, to the intersection between University Boulevard and Greensboro Avenue. Not only was the small force completely outnumbered, but even their artillery had been captured by the enemy forces on the bridge.

Realizing that the situation was hopeless, President Landon Garland ordered Colonel Murfree to return the cadets to the university, where they replenished their supplies, including their blankets, overcoats and hardtack. At 2:00 a.m. the next morning, the cadets and many of the faculty left the university along Huntsville Road. The next day, General Croxton's Federal troops burned the university, sparing only the Gorgas House, the Old Observatory, Maxwell Hall and the President's Mansion.

People say that the President's Mansion would not even exist had it not been for the wife of President Landon Garland. On April 4, 1865, the university's first lady, Louisa Frances Garland, had taken shelter at Bryce Hospital when she learned that the Union army was burning the university. She became infuriated as she rode past the burning buildings in her buggy. By the time she arrived at the mansion, a company of Union soldiers was setting fire to a pile of furniture inside the house. As the flames began consuming the carpet, Mrs. Garland stamped across the pine floor and ordered one of the young men to put out the flames. Taken aback by Mrs. Garland's stunning

On April 4, 1865, Louisa Frances Garland prevented a company of Union soldiers from burning down the President's Mansion on the University of Alabama's campus. *Alan Brown.*

beauty and bold act of defiance, the soldiers helped her douse the flames. The virtual campus tour on the University of Alabama's website reads, "Her strength of will and presence of mind stopped the Federal Army from destroying the mansion, and the young Union soldiers even worked to put out the fire they had already started at the place."

Over the years, the President's Mansion has been renovated several times, and the old house assumed its present appearance, with three stories and white stucco brick, in 1908. The centrally placed double staircase is used to access the upper two floors. The front façade, which is five bays wide, is fronted by a hexastyle portico designed in the Ionic style.

THE LEGENDS OF ATHENS STATE UNIVERSITY'S FOUNDERS HALL

The oldest building on the Athens State University campus is Founders Hall. Sandra Cook, who works in the President's Office, said that the entire community supported the construction of the building in 1822 because "they wanted a place where their girls could become Southern belles." The four massive columns in the front of the building were named Matthew, Mark, Luke and John, probably because, at the time, it was under the auspices of the Methodist Church, where it remained until 1975. According to the earliest of the university's legends, one of the brick masons was in the habit of taking an occasional "nip" of whiskey while working on the columns. One day, he was enjoying his afternoon libation when his supervisor walked by. Panic-stricken, he dropped his keg of whiskey inside one of the four columns. Before the workman could retrieve it, one of his fellow workers completed work on the column, forever concealing the keg from its rightful owner.

Another of Athens State University's signature legends dates back to the Civil War. The Union army viewed Athens as an important military target because it was the site of an important depot on the Nashville and Decatur Railroad. On April 26, 1862, two Ohio units occupied Athens, where many citizens were Union sympathizers. In fact, they had even burned Alabama's secessionist senator William Lowndes Yancey in effigy. For five days, relations between Federal troops and the people of Athens were peaceful. However, the fragile peace was shattered on May 1, 1862, when the Confederate First Louisiana Cavalry temporarily liberated Athens. Some of the members of the Eighteenth Ohio Brigade, under the command of General John Turchin, swore that the citizens of Athens had fired on them during their retreat. When the Ohio units returned to Athens the next day, they were hungry for revenge. The Eighth Brigade, under the command of Colonel John Turchin, believed Ormsby M. Mitchel sanctioned the sacking of Athens. After stacking their rifles on the courthouse lawn, the soldiers proceeded to the town's business district, where they vandalized the Cumberland Presbyterian Church, robbed William S. Allen's drugstore and destroyed his library, stole $3,000 worth of food from Madison Thompson's grocery store, pillaged Peterson Tanner and Sons Dry Goods store and accosted women. Two of Turchin's soldiers were accused of raping a fourteen-year-old slave girl belonging to Charlotte Hines. Afterward, Colonel Turchin was court-martialed and found guilty of dereliction of duty. Ironically, though, he was eventually promoted to general.

The foremost legend to emerge from Athens's tragic Civil War years is that of Madame Jane Hamilton Childs's confrontation with the Union army. The former head of Huntsville Female College was appointed president in 1856. In her first official act as president, she renamed the school the Athens Collegiate Institute. Miraculously, she was able to keep the school open and functioning until the end of the war. Students attended classes, and locals attended musicals performed at the college. She is best known today as the woman who saved Founders Hall from destruction. The story goes that on May 2, 1862, Colonel Turchin ordered his men to rest their horses on the lawn of the girls' college. He then climbed the steps of Founders Hall and was met at the door by Madame Childs, who produced a letter from the folds of her skirt. After reading the letter, Turchin stood at attention, saluted Madame Childs and ordered his soldiers to guard the college during the extent of the siege. Supposedly, the letter was a note from President Abraham Lincoln stating that the school must be saved at any cost.

Needless to say, the story of Madame Childs's heroic stand against the Union army endeared her to the entire state of Alabama. However, at least two historians have labeled the tale as being nothing more than a legend. Elva Bell McLin, author of *ASC History: 1821–1994*, said that Madame Childs could have gotten the letter through the connections she made in Washington, D.C., when she operated a school for girls in Georgetown. Athens State archivist Sara Love believes that Madame Childs got the letter from the U.S. secretary of war, Edward Stanton, who was married to her best friend. Love believes that Stanton could have written the letter himself or he could have gotten one from Lincoln. Some skeptics assert that the girls' college was spared from destruction, not because of a letter from Abraham

On May 2, 1862, Madame Jane Hamilton Childs prevented Colonel John Turchin's soldiers from burning Founders Hall by showing him a letter written by Abraham Lincoln. *Dpepper73.*

Lincoln, but because Founders Hall was used as a stop on the Underground Railroad. In fact, a room in the cellar would have been an ideal place to conceal fugitive slaves. For the time being, the legend of Founders Hall's survival remains just that—a legend. Generations of librarians have scoured the archives in search of Lincoln's letter, but none has had success.

THE COVERED BRIDGE AT THE UNIVERSITY OF WEST ALABAMA

At first glance, the architecture of the University of West Alabama appears similar to that of every other state university. What sets it apart from Alabama's other institutions of higher learning is its covered bridge. The Alamuchee-Bellamy Covered Bridge is one of the oldest covered bridges still existing in Alabama. Construction of the eighty-eight-foot-long bridge was supervised by Confederate army captain William Alexander Campbell Jones. It originally spanned the Sucarnochee River, and in 1865, the Confederate forces of General Nathan Bedford Forrest used the bridge as an access route to Mississippi. In 1924, the bridge was relocated five miles farther south to the old Bellamy-Livingston Road (now CR 13). It was given the name "Alamuchee Covered Bridge" because it crossed the Alamuchee Creek. The bridge was used for motor traffic until 1958, when a lumber truck crashed through the floor. The Alamuchee-Bellamy Covered Bridge was closed and left unmaintained until 1971, when the Sumter County Historical Society moved the bridge to the university's duck pond and restored it to its original appearance. The wheelchair-accessible bridge is used almost exclusively by students walking across campus. Many of these students still speak of the legend of Sumter County's outlaw sheriff who not only crossed the bridge almost daily but who lost his life very close to it.

Born in Georgia in 1843, Steve Renfroe served in Company G of the Ninth Alabama Infantry Regiment from 1861 to 1864. He married Mary E. "Mollie" Shepard on September 2, 1865, and lived in Butler County, Alabama, until he was forced to flee to Lowndes County, Alabama, after shooting his brother-in-law. In 1868, he moved to Sumter County and used his wife's family connections to join the Ku Klux Klan. Following Mollie's death in 1868, Steve married Mary M. "Pattie" Sledge. Two years later, Pattie died, and Steve buried her at Old Sides Cemetery. Later on, he had Mollie's body exhumed from Bethel Cemetery at Sumterville and re-buried next to Pattie. He married his third wife, Cherry V. Reynolds, in 1873. While he was a member of the Ku Klux Klan, Renfroe and his cronies were instrumental in the persecution of local African Americans, the disappearance of a Republican judge and the murder of a local magistrate. Two years after a jury found him innocent in the murder of a carpetbagger named Billings in 1874, Renfroe was elected sheriff of Sumter County.

Unfortunately, Steve Renfroe proved to be a poor administrator. After a few months in office, he was charged with embezzlement of county funds and thrown into his own jail. That night, he broke down the jail door, set all of the other prisoners free and burned down the county clerk's office, which contained his indictment papers. He was arrested, in spite of his friends' attempts to persuade him to leave town, and returned to jail. However, when the jailer discovered that he had nearly cut though the bars in the jailhouse window with a hacksaw blade, he was transferred to the jail in Tuscaloosa, which was allegedly much stronger. A few days later, Renfroe burned a hole in the eighteen-inch-thick pine floor and escaped again. He fled to Slidell, Louisiana, where he was apprehended and sentenced to hard labor in the mines of the Pratt Coal and Iron Company in Birmingham. In less than sixty days, Renfroe escaped by walking backward down a creek to elude the bloodhounds. He eventually made his way to the "Flat Woods" between Livingston and the Mississippi border. From his hideout, Renfroe proceeded to rob plantation homes and houses in small towns. Renfroe remained there until the summer of 1886, when he was captured on July 10 by three men in Enterprise, Mississippi, and returned by train to Livingston on July 13. That evening, eight men entered the jail, took the keys from the jailer and opened Renfroe's cell. They led him down through a cow pasture to the banks of the Sucarnochee River, where they lynched him from a chinaberry tree. No one in the lynch mob was ever arrested, and their identities remain unknown to this day.

Afterward, the jailer and sheriff cut Renfroe down and placed his body on a cot in the courthouse. Passersby claimed they saw a green glow hovering over the rotunda. The next day, Renfroe was buried in a potter's field by the railroad track. Legend has it that his brother-in-law exhumed Renfroe's corpse a few months later and buried him in Old Sides Cemetery between his first two wives, Mollie and Pattie. Carl Carmer, the author of *Stars Fell on Alabama*, writes that on every July 13 at 8:30 p.m., Renfroe's ghost can be seen sitting astride his horse Death before riding out of the clouds, swooping over the Sucarnochee River and flying back into the sky. Legends about the hanging tree have also been told for many years. People say that birds will not nest in its branches and that cows will not rest under the shade of its

The Alamuchee Covered Bridge was relocated to the University of West Alabama's campus in 1971. Locals believe that the spirits of two African American men who were murdered by Steve Renfroe, the "Outlaw Sheriff of Sumter County," haunt the old bridge. *Alan Brown.*

limbs. The most persistent legend was told to local folklorist Ruby Pickens Tartt in the 1930s by ex-slave Henry Gary. According to Gary, if someone were to knock on the hanging tree and say, "Renfroe, Renfroe, what did you do?" the tree would reply, "Nothing."

The chinaberry tree that served as a temporary hanging tree was located very close to the Alamuchee-Bellamy Covered Bridge. For this reason, many students claim to have seen Renfroe's ghost walking or riding his mule over the old bridge. Some of the older members of the community believe that Renfroe murdered two African American men on the Sucarnochee Bridge. Consequently, many students refuse to walk across the bridge for fear of running into their restless spirits. The truth is that in 1868, Steve Renfroe shot and killed Caesar Davis and Frank Sledge on an old iron bridge—the "Bridge at Boyd"—not the Alamuchee-Bellamy Covered Bridge. This is a good example of a legend that, through various retellings, has been relocated from one site to another.

The Strange History of Auburn University's War Eagle

Since 1979, Auburn University has been represented during football games by Aubie, the school's official mascot. The playful tiger has endeared himself to fans and players so much that the Universal Cheerleaders Association voted Aubie the number one collegiate mascot in the United States in 1991, 1995, 1996, 2003, 2006 and 2012. However, many people mistakenly believe that Auburn University has a second—and much older—mascot, War Eagle, which is not a mascot at all. It is a battle cry. The origin of War Eagle is shrouded in legend and speculation.

For years, faculty and students accepted the theory that the eagle was named after the Native Americans of the plains who used feathers in their war bonnets. Then in 1959, Jim Phillips wrote a much more fanciful backstory in the editorial page of the *August Plainsman*. During the Battle of the Wilderness in 1864, a wounded Confederate soldier was limping through the battlefield, trying to avoid stepping on the dead and dying soldiers who were on the ground, when he found an injured eagle. The soldier took pity on the bird and carried him off the battlefield. He named the eagle Anvre and made the bird his pet. After the war, the former soldier became a professor at Auburn University, and Anvre accompanied his master everywhere he went on campus. In 1892, the faculty member and his beloved bird were watching a football game against the University of Georgia when the excited crowd, spurred on by the presence of its good-luck bird, began chanting "War Eagle." Just as the Auburn team made the winning play, the aged eagle flew away from his master and soared over the crowd before dropping to the ground, dead.

Another mythical explanation for the War Eagle chant takes place during a football game against the Carlisle Indians in 1914. The Indians' most formidable player was a huge lineman and tackle whom everyone called "Bald Eagle." In an effort to wear him out, the Auburn team began running all of their plays against his position. Instead of calling the plays in the huddle, the quarterback, Lucy Hairston, simply yelled "Bald Eagle." The fans, whose hearing was obscured by all of the cheering, thought that the quarterback was actually yelling "War Eagle," so they too picked up the chant. In another version of the tale, the Carlisle fans and players began yelling "War Eagle" every time their team scored. However, when Lucy Hairston scored the winning touchdown, he took up the Indians' battle cry.

The most plausible origin story for "War Eagle" was published in 1998 in an article in the *Auburn Plainsman*. In 1913, a pep rally was held the day before the game against the University of Georgia. Cheerleader Gus Graydon tried to "pump up" the fans by proclaiming, "If we are going to win this game, we'll have to get out there and fight, because this means war." In the midst of all the cheering, a student dressed in a military uniform, E. T. Enslen, looked down from his seat in the bleachers and noticed that the metal emblem had come loose and fallen from his hat. When a friend asked him what he found, the young soldier yelled "It's a War Eagle" loud enough to be heard over the roar of the other fans. The next day, fans adopted "War Eagle" as their battle cry during the game against Georgia.

"War Eagle" was already firmly established as the university's battle cry when fourteen of Auburn's citizens paid a farmer ten dollars for a golden eagle that had become ensnared in a tangle of pea vines while attempting to swoop down on a flock of turkeys in Bee Hive, Alabama, in November 1930. The injured eagle was nursed back to heath by two cheerleaders, DeWit Stier and Harry "Happy" Davis. The bird was enclosed in a steel cage and taken to the Auburn football game against the University of South Carolina on Thanksgiving Day by the "A" Club. Auburn fans believed that the Tigers pulled off an unexpected win against their favored rival largely due to the presence of War Eagle II, as the bird became known. No one really knows what happed to War Eagle II following the game. Some say that students

A golden eagle known as "War Eagle" is the unofficial mascot of Auburn University. *J. Glover—Atlanta, Georgia.*

from a rival school stole the bird. Others say that a zoo bought War Eagle II. In a third variant of the tale, War Eagle II died and was stuffed and placed in the John Bell Lovelace Athletic Museum. In her book *Alabama: One Big Front Porch*, author Kathryn Tucker Windham wrote that War Eagle II was given to a traveling carnival that had stopped in Auburn. At the time of writing this book, War Eagle II has been succeeded by six other unofficial mascots. To this day, Auburn University still does not refer to War Eagle as a mascot even though the eagle plays an important role in the team's pregame activities at Jordan-Hare Stadium.

XI
LEGENDARY CHARACTERS

MOBILE'S RUNAWAY PRINCESS

Mobile was established by the French in 1702. The first settlement thrived largely due to the fur trade with the Native Americans. The French communicated with the Native Americans using a specialized trade language called Mobile jargon, which disappeared in the mid-1800s following the removal of the native population. Mobile prospered under French rule until 1763, when the British defeated the French in the French and Indian War. One of Mobile's most enduring legends is set in the French colonial period.

According to Peter J. Hamilton, author of *Colonial Mobile: An Historical Study*, the son of Peter the Great married a young woman named Catherine. Because he was physically and verbally abusive to her, Catherine decided to leave her husband by faking her own death. Not long after she was interred, her friends broke into her tomb and helped her escape. Catherine eventually boarded a ship with two hundred immigrants and made her way to the port of Mobile. She had not been in Mobile for very long when she caught the eye of a French officer named D'Aubant. He struck up a conversation with the young woman and told her that he believed he had seen her when he was stationed in St. Petersburg. He then asked if she was the daughter-in-law of Peter the Great, and she said that she was. Over the next few weeks, D'Aubant and Catherine fell in love and were married. The couple are said to have planted two oak trees while D'Aubant was stationed at Fort Conde in Mobile. Both of the trees are still standing.

In 1759, D'Aubant informed his wife that he was being transferred from the fort at Mobile to Fort Toulouse near the present town of Wetumpka, where he was chosen to replace Montberaut as commander. The story goes that he kissed his wife and little daughter goodbye and promised to have them brought to their home soon. By the time June arrived, Catherine had become impatient to be reunited with her husband. She and her child boarded a small boat and traveled up the river to Fort Toulouse. When they finally arrived at the fort, D'Aubant was both surprised and overjoyed to see them. The soldiers immediately set about building a cabin for D'Aubant and his family. Remnants of their cabin were visible for many years on the outskirts of Wetumpka. After a few years, D'Aubant returned to France accompanied by his wife and daughter.

Hamilton reluctantly rejects the legend of the French soldier and the Russian princess. He says that D'Aubant's real wife was Louise Marguerite of the prominent Bernoudy family. She died in 1759 and was buried in a church in Mobile. "It seems a pity the story may not be true, for it is romantic and interesting, but the church records can hardly be gainsaid."

Carl Carmer, author of *Stars Fell on Alabama*, put his own slant on the story. He said that after D'Aubant and Catherine sailed for France, it was later discovered that Catherine was a fraud. She was actually a servant to the wife of Alexei Petrovich. After stealing the royal jewels, she fled to America and assumed her identity. Carmer ends his account of the legend by saying, "So Mobile provided America with a legend of a Russian princess long before the days of Anastasia."

Here Comes the Goat Man!

American history is populated with fascinating figures who became legends in their own time. Daredevils like Evel Knievel immediately come to mind. Johnny Appleseed became a folkloric figure long before his own death, and Davy Crockett intentionally embellished his personal exploits in order to improve his chances of being elected senator. A more recent example of a person who was a "legend in his own time" was Charles "Chess" McCartney, otherwise known as the "Goat Man."

McCartney was born in Sigourney, Iowa, in 1901. He told an interviewer that he ran away from home when he was fourteen and traveled to New York, where he married a woman who was twenty-four years old. They worked as a team at circuses and sideshows. She was a Spanish knife thrower, and he was her target. After two years, he returned to Iowa and took up farming. In 1929, following the stock market crash, McCartney lost his farm. One day, a tree fell on top of him and crushed the left side of his body. The doctor pronounced him dead, and he was taken to a mortuary. To the undertaker's surprise, McCartney rose up from the table and began looking around.

McCartney eventually recovered from his injuries and took to the road as an itinerant preacher. He traveled in an iron-wheeled goat cart loaded down with objects he had found along the way, such as pots, pans, license plates, lanterns, a bed and even a potbellied stove, which he sold to finance his travels. Some people say that his wife traveled with him for a while and made clothes for her family from goat skins. Others say that he sold his wife to a neighbor for $1,000. In yet another version of the tale, she returned to Iowa with their son, who was raised by McCartney's parents. During his travels, McCartney claimed to have been married two more times and to have fathered four sons and a daughter. In 1988, the body of McCartney's son Gene was found in an old bus in Twiggs County, Georgia, where he and his father had lived for a while. He had been shot to death.

Between 1930 and 1987, McCartney walked one hundred thousand miles in forty-nine states and Canada, but he preferred the South because of the warm weather. At one time, he had as many as thirty goats pulling his rickety cart. McCartney told a reporter for the *Rome News-Tribune* in Georgia that he drank goat's milk and slept with his goats to keep warm on chilly nights. Thousands of people thronged to see the colorful preacher, although the strong goat smell compelled many to keep their distance. The Goat Man is said to have caused traffic jams along the old Dixie Highway running through Kentucky, Tennessee, Georgia and Florida. Toward the end of his life, he became nationally famous and had the opportunity to meet presidents and book a spot on *The Johnny Carson Show*. As his fame grew, so did his accounts of his adventurous life. In his many interviews, McCartney said that he had wrestled a bear and had almost been lynched by the Ku Klux Klan. He even claimed to have been beaten while trying to catch a glimpse of actress Morgan Fairchild in Los Angeles.

In the late 1960s, McCartney led his goat cart into Alabama. A NASA photographer named Durrell Bouldin photographed the Goat Man's visits to Albertville. At the time, McCartney had set up camp in a wooded area near the Albertville Regional Airport in Marshall County. Following Durrell

Bouldin's death, his son Charles posted his father's previously unpublished photographs on his website. The Goat Man was also photographed in places like Madison and Mobile.

McCartney died in a nursing home in Macon, Georgia, on November 15, 1998. Although his age is officially registered as 97, some people believe that he was 120 years old when he died. By the time of his death, the "Goat Man" was so well known that the *New York Times* published his obituary.

LOU WOOSTER: THE MADAM WHO SAVED BIRMINGHAM

William Wooster, an engineer from New York, lived in Tuscaloosa with his wife, Mary Chisolm Wooster, and their eight daughters. The couple's fifth daughter, Louise Catherine Wooster, was born in 1842. Following William's death in 1851, Mary Wooster married a man named John Williams. After a few years of marriage, Williams stole all of Mary's money and left her and her children destitute. After Mary died, her children were orphaned, and on the day following Mary's funeral, March 16, 1857, the youngest girls were sent to Mobile's Protestant Orphan Asylum. One of the oldest girls, Margaret, was married three times before opening a brothel on Third Avenue North under the name "Maggie Bracken." Lou and her sister were sent to live with their older sister, Frances Van Buren, who lived in New Orleans with her husband. When Mr. Van Buren refused Lou's plea to have her sisters released from the orphanage, she traveled by ship to Mobile and made her way to the orphanage, where she forged Frances's signature and secured her sisters' release on April 15, 1857.

Lou and her sisters moved in with a family friend, Robert A. Harris, in Mobile. In her book *The Autobiography of a Magdalen* (1911), Lou claimed that Harris initiated her moral decline by seducing her when she was fifteen years old. When her stepfather learned that she and her sisters were living with Harris, he traveled to Mobile and retrieved the girls back to New Orleans. For a while, Lou worked as a shop girl in New Orleans, but she soon returned to Mobile and moved back in with Harris. While in Mobile, Lou contracted yellow fever. While Harris abandoned her, another male friend took her to a local brothel where, Lou wrote, she "fell, step by step, until at last [she] was beyond redemption."

Because her family was still known in Mobile, Lou decided to preserve their reputation by moving to Montgomery, where she worked in a brothel. She had close relationships with several men at this time, one of whom almost drove her to suicide after he was killed in a shootout. In her autobiography, Lou claimed that in 1861, she was romantically involved with John Wilkes Booth. In fact, she proclaimed that she gave up on romance entirely after Booth broke off their love affair. Years later, Lou tried to capitalize on her relationship with the notorious assassin by showing newspaper reporters various mementoes she had received from Booth, including an unsigned letter. She said that because of Booth's influence, she became an actress, performing briefly in Arkansas and New Orleans before a bout of tuberculosis forced her to abandon her acting career and return to Mobile in 1869.

Lou entered an entirely new stage of her life when she moved to the relatively new city of Birmingham. While there, she resumed her career as a lady of the evening. That same year, Birmingham suffered from a devastating cholera epidemic during which approximately 50 percent of the city's population fled for fear of contracting the dreaded disease. The local hospital was stretched beyond its limits, and many people would have died untreated had not Lou and several of the women she worked with volunteered to enter the homes of people suffering from the disease. They risked their lives nursing the sick and preparing the dead for burial. Lou claimed that she not only devoted her time to the eradication of the disease, but she dedicated all of her money as well. After the epidemic finally ended, Dr. Mortimer Johnson paid homage to Lou and the other prostitutes in his official report by praising the "women of the town" for their selfless assistance during the city's time of need.

Once the cholera epidemic had subsided, Lou returned to Mobile. For ten years, she operated a "boarding house," which might have been a euphemism for a brothel. Lou worked as a prostitute with her youngest sister, Cornelia, who had a son. Lou paid scant attention in her autobiography to her time in Montgomery between 1873 and 1884. She hinted that she had suffered mightily in this decade, especially between 1876 and 1882, when she was brutalized by a male acquaintance in Montgomery.

In 1884, Lou returned to Birmingham once again, where she set up a brothel at 1914–16 Fourth Avenue North. Seven other women and a servant named Lucretia Bell resided at her "boarding house." Her business was so successful that she bought the building next to hers for $12,000. Her sister Cornelia and her sickly son lived in this building, and Lou continued to work in the other one until she retired in 1901. Seven years later, Lou

According to local legend, a procession of carriages with no passengers attended Louise Wooster's graveside service at Oak Hill Cemetery in 1913. *Alan Brown.*

rented her buildings to other businesses and moved into a modest house in Birmingham's southside. She succumbed to an attack of Bright's disease on May 16, 1913, just before her seventy-first birthday.

Lou Wooster was fondly remembered for her philanthropy by many of Birmingham's citizens. Not only did she provide invaluable assistance to the city in the dark days of 1873, but in 1887, she also donated $100 to a charity hospital campaign. Toward the end of her life, she arranged for the burial of several prostitutes and their babies next to her own plot in Oak Hill Cemetery. The story goes that on the day of her funeral, a long procession of carriages paraded down the main streets of Birmingham. However, many of the carriages had no passengers. Rumors soon spread that a number of the city's most prominent men felt obliged to pay their respects to one of Birmingham's most notorious women, but they did not want to admit that they knew her personally, so they arranged for their carriages to participate in the funeral procession while they stayed at home.

MARIA FEARING: THE SLAVE-TURNED-MISSIONARY

American history is populated with heroic women who triumphed over adversity. Some of the most stirring stories are those of female ex-slaves who achieved fame despite growing up in chains. Harriet Tubman was born in slavery in 1822. Following her escape, she embarked on seventy missions to free seventy slaved people, some of whom were her friends and family members. Harriet Jacobs was born a slave in 1813. The sexual harassment by her master drove her to hide in her grandmother's attic for seven years before escaping to Philadelphia, Pennsylvania. Jacobs recounted her struggles as a slave and as a free woman in her ex-slave narrative, *Incidents in the Life of a Slave Girl.* A much less famous example of a courageous African American woman who exceeded all of life's expectations for her is Maria Fearing.

Maria Fearing was born on a plantation owned by William O. Winston near Gainesville, Alabama, on July 26, 1838. She was more fortunate than many female slaves because she did not have to labor in the fields. Maria was a house slave who cared for her master's children. Growing up as a slave, Maria and the other children in the household learned about the Bible,

Presbyterian catechism and tales of the work of missionaries in Africa from her mistress, Amanda Fearing.

Following the end of the Civil War, Maria adopted the surname of her former owner, Fearing. Although she was already in her thirties before she was fully emancipated, Fearing was determined to realize her dream of becoming a missionary. She learned to read and write when she was thirty-three years old. After that, she got a job and earned a teaching degree from the Freedman's Bureau School in Talladega.

For several years, Fearing worked as a teacher in Calhoun County. Then in 1891, Fearing's life was changed forever after she heard a speech by a Presbyterian minister named William Sheppard at Talladega College. When she was fifty-six years old, Fearing applied to the Presbyterian Church to be accepted as a missionary to the Congo. When her application was denied, she decided to finance her own missionary work. She sold her house in May 1894, and the Congregational church in Talladega designated a contribution of $100 as support for Fearing's trip to Africa. She booked passage on a ship from New York to the Congo and embarked on a two-month-long journey to the mission station at Luebo along with three other African American missionaries. She worked without pay for two years before finally being granted a salary. While in Luebo, Fearing established the Pantops Home for Girls where young women, who had previously been orphans and slaves, were taught reading, writing, arithmetic and the basic tenets of the Christian faith. She was known by her young charges as *mama wa Mputu* or "mother from far away."

Fearing worked for the people of the Congo for twenty years before she was forced to retire from missionary service for health reasons in 1915 when she was seventy-eight years old. The Southern Presbyterian Church awarded her the Loving Cup in 1918. Fearing continued her teaching career in Selma before she retired and returned to Sumter County, Alabama, where she died at age ninety-nine.

Railroad Bill: Alabama's Shape-Shifting Outlaw

Little is known about the early life of the outlaw who came to be known as Railroad Bill. According to an article published in the *Montgomery Daily Advertiser* on April 10, 1895, he earned a living as a circus performer before becoming a convict lease worker in the turpentine camps of Bluff Springs, Florida. During this time, he went by the name of Morris Slater, but he acquired the nickname "Railroad Time" because he was a speedy worker. In 1893, he got into an argument with a sheriff in Florida for carrying a rifle without a license. Slater resisted arrest and shot the deputy. "Railroad Bill," as the sheriff's deputies referred to Slater, fled the turpentine camps and embarked on a life of crime. He organized a band of robbers whose primary targets were freight cars loaded down with cargo. Their *modus operandi* involved placing a man inside the freight car at night who would wait for the train to leave the station before throwing cans of food onto the tracks, which the other gang members picked up. Railroad Bill was viewed by many African Americans as a Robin Hood–type figure because he sold the cans of food to them at reduced prices.

Over the next year, Railroad Bill was transformed into a folkloric figure. People said he was a voodoo doctor who could change himself into an animal. Supposedly, Railroad Bill eluded a sheriff's posse by transforming himself into a sheep. During another manhunt, Railroad Bill changed into a brown, short-haired dog that joined the pack of hounds that were chasing him. He was also reputed to be able to inhibit the tracking abilities of the bloodhounds on his trail. A white hunter accidentally made Railroad Bill's acquaintance when he fired his gun at a small fox. The man swore that he heard a laugh as the animal scampered away. As the stories of his miraculous escapes began to spread, locals began spreading the rumor that he was impervious to all but silver bullets.

The search for Railroad Bill escalated in 1895 when on March 6, a crew of railroad workers took Bill's rifle and pistol while he was sleeping behind a water tank. Suddenly, Bill leapt to his feet and began shooting at the men with another pistol he had hidden on his person. He escaped by hopping aboard an oncoming train. On April 6, 1895, a posse surrounded a barn where Railroad Bill was hiding. One of the members of the posse, James Stewart, was shot and killed in the ensuing gunfight, and Railroad Bill was able to sneak out of the barn amid all of the confusion. On April 12, 1895, a posse accidentally shot and killed Mark Stinson in a cabin where Railroad Bill was known to spend the night. Stinson was a confidante of Railroad Bill's who was working as an undercover agent at the time.

Railroad Bill's fate was sealed following his shooting of Sheriff Edward S. McMillan of Brewton, Alabama. McMillan was the leader of a posse that tracked Railroad Bill to a cabin near Bluff Springs. Railroad Bill fired his rifle at his pursers, fatally wounding McMillan. When he realized what he had done, Railroad Bill ran into the woods.

Following the high-profile murder of Sheriff McMillan, the reward for his capture was raised to $1,250. For a while, this caused an "open season" on African American males in the Deep South, and many were beaten and whipped by bounty hunters from places as far away as Texas and Indiana. Newspapers reported the killing of an untold number of African American men who were misidentified as Railroad Bill in Mississippi, Florida, Georgia and Texas. Eventually, Pinkerton agents and L&N Railroad detectives joined in the hunt for Railroad Bill.

Railroad Bill's criminal career came to an abrupt end in Atmore, Alabama, on March 7, 1896. On this particular day, he was hunkered down in an old shack. He left the safety of his hiding place and walked over to Tidmore's store to purchase supplies. Unknown to Railroad Bill, one member of a two-man posse, R.C. John, was squatting behind the counter with rifle in hand. While the outlaw was talking to the owner of the store, John jumped up from behind the counter and shot Railroad Bill twice in the back. He staggered toward the door and collapsed in a heap. John's partner, Leonard McGowin, walked over to Railroad Bill's body and fired his shotgun, blowing off a large portion of his head.

Railroad Bill's corpse was transported to Montgomery for identification. Onlookers were charged twenty-five cents a head to view his bullet-ridden remains. The body was put on display once again after it was taken to Pensacola, Florida. A few weeks later, the corpse was "petrified" in Birmingham in order to preserve it for permanent display. Railroad Bill was finally given a Christian burial in St. John's Cemetery in Pensacola on March 30, 1896.

The legacy of Railroad Bill stretches far beyond that of other outlaws from Alabama. In the early 1990s, a ballad celebrating the exploits of the African American outlaw began circulating throughout the Deep South. In the 1960s, folksingers like Joan Baez and Bob Dylan revived the old folk song:

> *Railroad Bill mighty bad man*
> *Shot all lights out brakeman's hand*
> *Was lookin' fer Railroad Bill*

People have also been inspired and entertained by tales of Railroad Bill's ill-gotten gains, none of which have ever been found. Many people have scoured the caves of southern Alabama and Florida in search of his loot. It is more likely, however, that he hid his money along the very railroad tracks that supplied him with his primary source of income.

WORKS CITED

Books

Beyerstein, Dale. "Edgar Cayce." In *Encyclopedia of the Paranormal*. Edited by Gordon Stein. N.p.: Prometheus Books, 1996, 146–53.

Brown, Alan. *The Haunting of Alabama*. Gretna, LA: Pelican Press, 2017.

Brunvand, Jan Howard. *The Vanishing Hitchhiker: American Urban Legends and their Meaning*. New York: W.W. Norton & Co., 2003.

Carmer, Carl. *Stars Fell on Alabama*. Tuscaloosa: University of Alabama Press, 1989.

Clanahan, James. *The History of Pickens Country, Alabama: 1540–1920*. Carrollton, AL: Clanahan Publications, 1964.

Cox, Dale. *Two Egg, Florida: A Collection of Ghost Stories, Legends and Unusual Facts*. N.p.: CreateSpace Independent Publishing Forum, 2007.

Davis, William C. *The Pirates Lafitte: The Treacherous World of the Corsairs of the Gulf*. New York: Harcourt Books, 2005.

Floyd, E. Randall. *Great Southern Mysteries*. New York: Barnes & Noble Books, 2000.

Fort, Charles. *The Book of the Damned*. New York: Ace Books, 1972.

Good, Timothy. *Above Top Secret*. New York: Quill, 1988.

Hamilton, Peter J. *Colonial Mobile: An Historical Study*. New York: Houghton Mifflin and Co., 1897.

Jemison, E. Grace. *Historical Tales of Talladega*. Talladega, AL: Talladega Press, 2010.

Massey, Larry. *Life and Crimes of Railroad Bill: Legendary African American Desperado*. Gainesville: University Press of Florida, 2015.

Michel, Aime. *The Truth about Flying Saucers*. New York: Criterion, 1956.

Miller, Elaine Hobson. *Myths, Mysteries, & Legends*. Birmingham, AL: Seacoast Publishing, 1995.

Mott, A.S. *Ghost Stories of Tennessee*. Auburn, WA: Lone Pine Publishing International, 2005.

Sterling, Robin. *Tales of Old Blount County*. N.p.: Lulu.com, 2013.

Stern, Jess. *The Sleeping Prophet*. New York: Bantam Books, 1967.

Sugrue, Thomas. *There Is a River*. N.p.: A.R.E. Press, 1997.

Taylor, Troy. *Season of the Witch*. Alton, IL: Whitechapel Productions Press, 1999.

Windham, Kathryn Tucker. *13 Alabama Ghosts and Jeffrey*. Tuscaloosa: University of Alabama Press, 1969.

Winer, Richard. *Ghost Ships*. New York: Berkely Books, 2000.

Magazine Articles

Cep, Casey N. "Harper Lee's Abandoned True-Crime Novel." *The New Yorker*. 17 March 2015.

Jones, Pam. "The Brasher-Dye Disappearance." *Alabama Heritage* 82 (Fall 2006).

Kellen, Erin. "In Hal's Kingdom." Alabama Folkways Articles. November 1993.

McLendon, Nancy Gregory. "Phantoms of the Wiregrass: Tracing the Incarnations of Alabama Folklore." *Alabama Heritage* (Fall 2011).

Penick, James. "Railroad Bill." *Gulf Coast Historical Review* 10, no. 1 (Fall 1994): 85–92.

Webster, James. "The Goat Man Visits Alabama." *Weird Alabama* 1 (2004).

Pamphlets

McQuiston, Debra, designer. *Ave Maria Grotto: Miniature Miracles*. Terrell Publishing Co., 2016.

Painter, Kath M., and Anna Thibodeaus. *Steamboats A-Landin'!* The Monroe County Heritage Museum, Monroeville, AL, 1992.

Spiegel, Mary Edith, teacher. *The History of Odenville, St. Clair County, Alabama*. The Commercial Art Class, 1932. Pellcitylibrary.com.

Newspapers

"Bell Witch Appears in Alabama–1912." *Montgomery Advertiser*. 25 February 1912.

Bryant, Walter. *Birmingham News*. 27 November 1975.

"Chasing History's Mysteries: The Legend of the Creature of the Coosa River." *Gadsden Messenger*. 29 March 2013.

"City Hall Sinking: The Immense Building Supposed to Be Sinking into the Ground." *Birmingham Age*. 7 May 1886.

"Ghosts or Gases? Tree Cries, Crowds Listen." *Kokomo (Ind.) Tribune*. 1 May 1981.

"Gold Buried during Civil War Days Unearthed Near Demopolis, Alabama." *Evening Independent*.1 June 1926.

"Here He Is! Henry Wells." *West Alabamian*. 30 January 1878.

Hollman, Holly. "Athens: 'The College that Lincoln Saved.'" *Decatur Daily*. 22 April 2005.

"Murder in Lowndes." *Daily Advertiser*. 29 December 1865.

Parsons, Carmel. "The Legend of Chewacla Creek." *Ledger-Enquirer East Alabama Today*. 9 May 1974.

Roney, Marty. "Creepy Discovery: Doll Display Pulled from Autauga Swamp." 25 November 2014.

"The Story behind Harper Lee's Lost True-Crime Novel." *New York Post*. 9 September 2015.

Interviews

Carter, Alice. Personal Interview. Conducted by Alan Brown, 2 February 2002.

Cooper, Hope. Personal Interview. Conducted by Alan Brown, 7 March 2003.

Morgan, Mike. Personal Interview. Conducted by Alan Brown, 5 April 2002.

Pearson, Garrett. Personal Interview. Conducted by Alan Brown, 29 November 2017.

Venable, Mary Ann. Personal Interview. Conducted by Alan Brown, 11 January 2003.

Works Cited

Websites

Abram, Susan. "Cherokees in Alabama." *Encyclopedia of Alabama.* www. encyclopediaofalabama.org/article/h-1087.

Alabamabigfootsociety.com. "A White Bigfoot Reported in Blount County, Alabama—Possible Albino." http://alabamabigfootsociety.com/ RecentSightings.html.

Alabama Communities of Excellence. "Alamuchee-Bellamy Covered Bridge." https://www.alabamacommunitiesofexcellence.org/attraction/ alamuchee-bellamy-covered-bridge

Alabama Women's Hall of Fame. "Alabama Women's Hall of Fame— Maria Fearing (1838–1937)." www.awhf.org>fearing.

Americanrivers.org. "Black Warrior River." https://www.americanrivers. org/river/black-warrior-river/.

Aminioapps.com. "The Wolf Woman of Mobile." http://aminoapps. com/;age/paranormal/7953371/the-wolf-woman-of-mobile.

Ancient Lost Treasures. "Whitfield Farm Treasure." www. ancientlosttreasures.com/forum/viewtopics.phys?f=197&t=1852.

Ancient Origins. "Leprechauns: At the End of the Rainbow Lies Richness for Irish Folklore." http://www.ancient-origins.net/news-myths-legends-europe/leprechauns-end-rainbow-lies-richness-irish-folklore-003920.

Arksey, Laura. "Chedwelah—Thumbnail History." Historylink.org. http:// www.historylink.org/File/9534.

Athens Plus. "Athens State Homecoming to Honor Legendary Madame Childs." http://www.athensplus.com/ASU_MadameChilds2012.htm.

Atkins, Leah Rawls. "Lake Martin and the Thomas Wesley Martin Dam." Encyclopedia of Alabama. http://www.encyclopediaofalabama.org/ article/h-1190.

Berntson, Ben. "Railroad Bill." Encyclopedia of Alabama. http://www. encyclopediaofalabama.org/article/h-1258.

Bhamwiki. "Underground River." http://www.bham.wiki.com/w/ Underground_river.

"Bigfoot of North America." *The Museum of Unnatural Mysteries.* http:// unmuseum.mus.pa.us/bigfoot.htm.

Brown, Melissa. "On This Day in 1865, Union Troops Burned the University of Alabama." Real-Time News from Birmingham. http:// www.al.com/news/birmingham/index.ssf/2015/04/on_this_day_ in_1865_unio_tro.html.

Burns, Phyllis Doyle. "Louisiana Werewolf—Rougarou of the Bayou." Exemplore.com. https://exemplore.com/cryptids/Louisiana-Werewolf-Rougarou-of-the-Bayou.

Calloway, Drew. "U.S. Air Force Releases Details about UFO Sightings in North Alabama." WHNT News 19. 21 January 2015. https://wjmt/cp,2015/01/21/united-states-air-force-releases-details-about-ufo-sightings-in-north-alabama.

Causey, Donna. "The Mystery of Hal's Lake—Clarke County, Alabama—How It Got Its Name." Alabama Pioneers. https://www.alabamapioneers.com/mystery-of-hals-lake.

———. "TBT: Is the City of Birmingham, Alabama Sitting above an Underground River that Connects with the Warrior River? There May Be Some Truth to This Story." Alabama Pioneers. http://alabamapioneers.com/is-birmingham-alabama-sitting-above-an-underground-river/.

Celtic-weddingrings.com. "Myth of the Leprechaun." https://www.celtic-weddingrings.com/celtic-mythology/myth-of-the-leprechaun.aspx.

Center, Clark E. "The Burning of the University of Alabama." *Alabama Heritage*. Spring 1990 (16): 30–45. https://www.alabamaheritage.com/alabama-heritage-blog/the-burning-of-ua-campus.

Charleyproject.org. "Ruth Purcell Murphree Dorsey." http://www.harleyhproject.org/cases/d/dorsey_ruth.html.

Clarke County Historical Museum. "Hal's Lake." https://www.clarkemuseum.com/html/hal_s_lake.html.

Conley, Mike. "Mike Conley's Tales of the Weird: Legend of the Wampus Cat." McDowell News. http://www.mcdowellnews.com/opinion/mike-conley-s-tales-of-the-weird-legend-of-the/article_3891ddce-f53e-5659-8126-e4274c9eb91.html.

Cox, Dale. "The Face in the Window." ExploreSouthernHistory.com. www.exploresouthernhistory.com.faceinthewindow.html.

———. "Two-Toed Tom—Alligator Monster of Florida and Alabama." ExploreSouthernHistory.com. http://www.exploresouthernhistory.com/alligator2html.

Crider, Beverly. "'Death Masks' of Mount Nebo Cemetery." http://blog.al.com/strange-alabama/2012/09/death_masks_of_mt_nebo_cemeter.html.

———. "Fort Morgan Mystery Ship Remains a Mystery." Al.com. http://blog.al.com/strange-alabama/2012/04/fort_morgan_mystery_ship_remai.html.

———. "The Goat Man: A Legend of Southern Folklore." AL.com. http://blog.al.com/strange-alabama/2012/04/the_goat_man_a_legend-of_south.html.

Cryptoville. "What Is a Rougarou, Exactly?" http://visitcryptoville.com/2014/04/01/what-is-a-rougarou-exactly/.

Cuthbert, Matt. "Oak Mountain Tunnel, Leeds, Alabama: Haunted by John Henry?" AL.com. https://www.al.com/goforth/04/oak_mountain_tunnel_leeds_alab.html.

Dailyoddsandends. "Lost Treasure of Alabama." https://dailyoddsandends.wordpress.com/2012/08/?lost-treasure-of-alabama/.

Davis, Robert Scott (2002). "The Georgia Odyssey of the Confederate Gold." *Georgia Historical Quarterly* 86, no. 4. https://www.jstor.org/stable/40584600.

Digging in the Dirt: The Search for My Roots. "Brasher Mystery #2." https://rootdiggers61.wordpress.com/2012/10/15/brasher-mystery-2/.

Digital Alabama. "Alabama Treasure Legends." www.digitalalabama.com.

Educating Humanity. "25 Years Ago, Tourists Descended on Tiny Alabama Town in Wake of UFO Sighting." http://www.educatinghumanity.com/2015/06/mass-ufo-sighting-alabama.html.

ExploreSouthernHistory.Com. "Noccalula Falls Park—Gadsden, Alabama." http://www.exploresouthernhistory.com/noccalula.htm.

Farris, David. "The Cherokee Legend of the Little People." Edmond Life & Leisure. http://edmondlifeandleisure.com/the-cherokee-legend-of-the-little-people-p10901-76htm.

Find a Grave Memorial. "Chief Tuskaloosa." http://www.findagrave.com/memorial/111626681/chief-tuskaloosa.

Firsttoknow.com. "The True Story of Ann Hodges: History's Only Meteorite Victim." http://firsttoknow.com/true-story-ann-hodges-historys-meteorite-victim?.

Freestateofwinston.org. "The Downey Booger." https://www.freestateofwinston.org/downeybooger.htm.

Garst, John. "On the Trail of the Real John Henry." History News Network. https://historynewsnetwork.org/Article/31137.

Gingeritch, Phillip D. "Basilosaurus cetoides." *Encyclopedia of Alabama.* www.encyclopediaofalabama.org/article/h-1386.

The Greenville Advocate. "Legend of the Wampus Cat: A Mountain Tradition." http://www.greenvilleadvocate.com/author/admin/.

Gryu, Jeremy. "A River Runs Through It? The Strange, Sometimes Fabricated Story of Birmingham's 'Mystic, Underground River.'" AL.com. http://blog.al.com/spotnews/2014?02/a_river_runs_through_it_the_st.html.

Hammons, Steve. "Cherokee Tales of the 'Little People' Give Clues about Our World." American Chronicle. http//www.bibliotecapleyades.net/arqueologia/esp-herokeetales.htm.

Hill, Emily. "Crichton Leprechaun Revisited: Meet the Man Who Discovered the Legend." AL.com. http://www.al.com/news/mobile/index.ssf/2015/03/crichton_leprechaun_revisited.html.

History.com. "Tecumseh—Native American History." www.history.com/topics/native-american-history/tecumseh.

Hoax.org. "The Disappearance of David Lang." http:/hoaxes.org.

Ignite the Underground. "Bear Creek Swamp." https://ignitetheunderground.wordpress.com/2011/10/24/bear-creek-swamp.

Ilhawaii.net. "Little People of the Cherokee." http://www.ilhawaii.net/-story/lore132htm.

Johnson, Ben. "The Discovery of America…by a Welsh Prince?" www.historic.uk.com/HistoryUK/HistoryofWales/The-discovery-of-America-by-Welsh-Prince.

Josegaspar.net. "The Legendary Jose Gaspar—Gasparilla, The Pirate." http://www.Josegaspar.net/index2.htm.

Kazek, Kelly. "Car-Sized Catfish? Supernatural Serpents? 'Monster Fish' Host Zeb Hogan Discusses Alabama's Legendary River Creatures." AL.com. http://www.al.com/living/index.ssf/2013/06/car-sized_catfish_supernatural.html.

———. "5 Mythical Creatures that Reportedly Roam Alabama's Back Roads." AL.com. http://www.al.com/living/index.ssf/2013/10/5_mythical_creatures_that_repo.html.

———. "Mystery of Alabama's Ancient Cave Caskets, Pine Boxes Built at the Asylum and the Coffin Shop." AL.com. http://www.al.com/living/index.ssf/2014/05/mystery_of_alabamas_ancient_ca.html.

———. "19th-Century Mooresville Psychic Was Known as 'X+Y=Z'" http://www.al.com/living/2012/10/19th-century_mooresville_psych.html.

———. "Remembering When the Goat Man Visited Alabama." AL.com. http://al.com/living/index.ss/2017/03/remembering_when_the_goat_man.html.

———. "Vanished: The South's Most Bizarre Disappearances." http://www.al.com/living/index.ssf/2015/09/vanished_the_souths_strangest.html.

Kelly, Brian. "Wreck of Sailing Ship Reappears at Fort Morgan Beach after Hurricane Isaac." AL.com. http://blog.al.com/live/2012/09/mystery_shipwreck_at_fort_morg.html.

Knowyourmeme.com. "Mobile Leprechaun." http://knowyourmeme.
com/memes/mobile-leprechaun.

Lalo, Lillian. "More Than 4,000 People Buried under Birmingham
Zoo and Botanical Gardens." WIAT CBS 42. http://wiat.
com/2015/04/28/more-than-4000-people-buried-under-birmingham-
zoo-and-botanical-gardens/.

Leepeacock2010.blogspot. "The Evergreen Courant's Flashback for
Jan. 28, 2013." http://leepeacock2010.blogspot.com/2013/01/the-
evergreen-courants-news-.

Marsh, Roger. "Football Field Sized UFO Stops Alabama I-20 Traffic."
OpenMinds. http://www.openminds.tv/football-field-sized-ufo-stops-
alabama-20-traffic/27921.

———. "Multiple Triangle UFOs Reported Low over Alabama."
OpenMinds. http://www.openminds.tv/multiple-triangle-ufos-reported-
low-over-alabama/34645flashback_28.html.

Mobile.Com. "Mobile Charm & History." http://mobile.org/mobile-
charm/history/.

Mysteriousuniverse.org. "Exploring American Monsters: Alabama." http://
mysteriousuniverse.org/2015/02/exploring-american-monsters-alabama/.

———. "The Tale of Two-Toed Tom, the Demon Gator." http://
mysteriousuniverse.org/2016/01/the-tale-of-two-toed-tom-the-demon-
gator/.

Mystery411.com. "Coosa River Monster." http://www.mystery411.com/
Landing_coosarivermonster.html.

Native-languages.org. "Native Languages of the Americas: Tsalagi/
Cherokee Legends, Myths, and Stories." http://native-languages.org/
Cherokee-legends.htm.

Newkirk, Greg. "Struck by Bad Luck: Meet the Woman Whose Life Was
Ruined by a Cursed Meteorite." Week in Weird. http://weekinweird.
com/2016/08/21/bad-luck-from-outer-space-meet-the-Woman-whose-
life-was-ruined-by-a-cursed-meteorite.

New-madrid.mo.us. "Strange Happenings during the Earthquakes." www.
new-madrid.mo.us/102/Earthquakes-of-1811-1812.

Paranormal-encounters.com. "The Louisiana Legend of the Rougarou."
http://paranormalencounters.com/wp/the-louisiana-legend-of-the-
rougarou/.

The Paranormal Pastor. "The Wolf Woman of Mobile, Alabama." http://
theparanormalpastor.blogspot.com/2009/08/wolf-woman-of-mobile-
alabama.html.

Paysinger, Christopher B. "Sack of Athens." Encyclopedia of Alabama. http://www.encyclopediaofalabama.org/article/h-1819.

Qst.net. "Unexplained Disappearances." http://qst.net/w5www/disappearances.html.

Radford, Benjamin. "Leprechauns: Facts about the Irish Trickster Fairy." Livescience.com. http://www.livescience.com/37626-leprechauns.html.

Raines, Ben. "Ancient Underwater Forest Off Alabama Is Much Older Than Scientists Thought." http://blog.al.com/wire/2013/03/ancient_underwater_forest_off.html.

Rainor, Joseph. "Spherical Grey UFO Sighted in Alabama." UFO Roundup. http://www.ufoinfo.com/roundup/v03/rnd03_35.html.

Ress, Thomas V. "Chewacla State Park." Encyclopedia of Alabama. www.encyclopediaofalabama.org/article/h-2574.

———. "Historic Blakeley State Park." Encyclopedia of Alabama. www.encyclopediofalabama.org/article/h-3034.

Roadside America. "Ave Maria Grotto." https://www.roadsideamerica.com/story/2015.

Rodriguez, Ana. "4,700 Remain Buried under Birmingham Zoo, Botanical Gardens, Lane Park." AL.com. http://www.al.com/news/birmingham/index.ssf/2015/03/post_221.html.

Rose, Christina. "Native: The Day Tecumseh's Prophecy Rocked the World." Indian Country Today. https://indiancountrymedianetwork.com/history/events/native-history-the-day-tecumsehs-prophecy-rocked-the-world/.

Roundtree, Shalonda. "Discovery of Unknown Cemeteries at Hunter Army Airfield Sheds Light on a Forgotten Past." The Society for Georgia Archaeology. Thesga.org/2009/org/discovery-of-unknown-cemeteries-at-Hunter-Army-Airfield-Sheds-light-on-a-forgotten-past.

RuralSWAlabama. "Isaac Nettles 'Death Masks' Headstones near Carlton, AL." https://www.ruralswalabama.org/attraction/Isaac-nettles-death-masks-headstones-near-carlton-al/.

Schlosser, S.E. "The Wampus Cat." American Folklore. http://americanfolklore.net/folklore/2010/08/the_wampus_cat.html.

Shearer, Rhonda Roland. "Alabama's Monster Pig Hoax, One Year Later." Imediaethics.org. http://www.imediaethics.org/alabamas-monster-pig-hoax-one-year-later?.

Smith, Ron. "Boll Weevil in Alabama." Encyclopedia of Alabama. www.encyclopediaofalabama.org/article/h-1436.

St. Clair County Bigfoot. "Stories of Alabama Bigfoot."
   http://saintclaircountybigfoot.wikifoundry.com/page/
   Stories+of+Alabama+Bigfoot.

Swancer, Brent. "The Tale of Two-Toed Tom, the Demon Gator." http://
   mysteriousuniverse.org.

Swope, Theresa. "Dorsey, Ruth, 8/17/1974." http://z10.invisionfree.
   com/usedtobedoe/ar/t2720.htm.

Toole, Connor. "What Is the Real Story behind the Legendary Alabama
   Leprechaun?" Funny Papers. http://elitedaily.com/humor/what-is-the-
   real-story-behind-the-legendary-alabama-leprechaun/.

Treasurenet.com. "Nunez Ferry Crossing—Perdido River AL/FL."

UFOs/Aliens.About.Com. "Alabama." http://ufos.about.com/library/
   bldata/b12alab.htm.

———. "UFOs: The Eastern Airlines Sighting." http://ufos.about.com/
   library/weekly/aa012798.htm.

Walesdirectory.co.uk. "Prince Madoc of Wales and the Discovery of
   America." www.walesdirectory.co.uk/Myths_and_legends/Prince_
   Madoc.htm.

Whitehead, Vera. "The Downey Booger." Freestateofwinston.org. https://
   www.freestateofwinston.org/downeybooger.htm.

Young, Greg. "Manhattan's Forgotten Graveyards, Under Public Parks,
   Famous Hotels and Supermarkets." Huffington Post. https://www.
   huffingtonpost.com/greg-young/manhattan-forgotten-graveyards_b_41.

Yourirish.com. "Legend of the Irish Leprechaun." http://www.yourirish.
   com/folklore/legend-of-leprechauns.

ABOUT THE AUTHOR

Alan Brown was born in Alton, Illinois, on January 12, 1950. After earning degress from Millikin University, Southern Illinois University, Illinois State University and the University of Illinois, he taught high school English in Flora and Springfield, Illinois. In 1986, he joined the English faculty at the University of West Alabama. When he is not teaching, Alan enjoys watching old movies, traveling with his wife, Marilyn, and spending time with his grandsons, Cade and Owen. Since publishing his first book, *Dim Roads and Dark Nights*, in 1993, he has explored his interest in folklore, especially ghost tales, in over thirty publications, including *Stories from the Haunted South* (2004), *Haunted Georgia* (2006), *Ghost Hunters of the South* (2006), *Ghost Hunters of New England* (2008), *Haunted Birmingham* (2009), *The Big Book of Texas Ghost Stories* (2010), *Haunted Meridian* (2011), *Ghosts along the Mississippi River* (2012), *Ghosts of Florida's Gulf Coast* (2014), *The Haunted South* (2014), *Ghosts of Mississippi's Golden Triangle* (2016), *The Haunted Southwest* (2016) and *The Haunting of Alabama* (2017).

Visit us at
www.historypress.com